The Self-Esteem Workbook for Women

THE SELF-ESTEEM WORKBOOK FOR WOMEN

5 STEPS TO GAINING CONFIDENCE AND INNER STRENGTH

MEGAN MacCUTCHEON, LPC

ALTHEA
PRESS

To all of the women who read this book:
It is my sincere hope that you find wisdom, self-discovery,
and inner strength that move you toward a more fulfilling future.

CONTENTS

INTRODUCTION

• • • • •

WELCOME TO *THE SELF-ESTEEM WORKBOOK FOR WOMEN!* Whether you picked up this book on your own or were given a copy by somebody who cares about your well-being, you are likely struggling with some type of challenge that is holding you back from living your best life. You may not readily identify your present struggles as being related to self-esteem; yet undoubtedly, you can benefit from something this book has to offer. This book is written specifically for women facing challenges associated with low self-esteem and for those looking to bolster their confidence and gain a greater level of inner strength. However, it can certainly be useful for any woman who feels a sense of discouragement or even just a lack of fulfillment in some area of her life.

For the past decade, I have studied and worked in the mental health field. I am currently a Licensed Professional Counselor with a private psychotherapy practice in Northern Virginia. I work primarily with adolescents and adults who are facing a variety of life challenges, and I regularly teach self-esteem-building workshops in my community. I have found that the tools useful for building self-esteem can benefit nearly anyone, regardless of what their struggles may be. The roots of things like depression and anxiety are often tied to problems with self-esteem or a poorly defined sense of identity. Therefore, tools used for boosting self-esteem can really be helpful for anyone who is interested in making positive changes in their life.

Self-esteem is a concept that impacts our lives in so many ways. It plays a role in how good or bad we feel about ourselves, how effectively we interact with others, and how successful we are in our life's endeavors. This book will provide valuable information about what self-esteem is, and more importantly, how the development of more positive self-esteem can help you lead a happier, more fulfilling life. I will share some case studies, real-life stories in which you will see the different ways low self-esteem can wreak havoc on people's lives. Through these stories you'll also get a glimpse into how a dedicated effort toward building self-esteem pays off in the long run. These stories involve real women I have personally worked with, though their names and identifying information have been changed to maintain confidentiality.

We are all unique individuals starting out at different places on our self-esteem journey. Everyone reading this book possesses their own cultural background, diverse past, life experiences, unique struggles, and varying initial levels of distress, uncertainty, and self-esteem. That said, I encourage you to work through the material at your own pace. View this process as your own personal journey in exploring your unique relationship with yourself and your self-esteem. Take as much time as you need in each section and with each exercise, based on your own individual situation and the time you can devote to putting these tools into practice.

Everyone can benefit from a boost in self-esteem, regardless of where they are starting out. No matter how high or low your self-esteem may be, you will find tools and information here that will help improve your overall quality of life. Through interactive questions, prompts, and exercises, you will have the opportunity to explore your own level of self-esteem. You will gain a better understanding of where low self-esteem stems from, and see how deficiencies in self-worth might be impacting various aspects of your life. Through the steps and tools offered, you will ultimately learn ways to build up your self-esteem and overcome many of the struggles you face in order to achieve a more satisfying life and future.

In the first chapter, we will explore what self-esteem is and what it is not. In chapter 2, we will look at specific issues that create and perpetuate low self-esteem for women. As we move through this book, we will explore a five-step program that can help you build self-esteem. These steps relate to and build upon one another and are relevant to all women, no matter where your self-esteem falls or what struggles you've endured in the past.

In the first step, you will get to know yourself better as you investigate your roots and discover how your current thoughts may keep you stuck in a place of low self-esteem. In step 2, you will discover ways to better care for yourself as you learn to banish self-doubt and lead a healthier life. Step 3 involves learning how to command the respect you deserve as you become more assertive (and perhaps less preoccupied with pleasing everyone else). In step 4, you will uncover the importance of accepting all aspects of yourself, as you learn to acknowledge weaknesses and forgive mistakes. In the final step, you will learn how to demonstrate love and compassion toward yourself. Here you'll also discover how self-love can not only improve your self-esteem but also create healthier, happier relationships that support a positive future.

Like many things, you'll get from this program what you put into it, so please take your time. Spend time applying what you've read to your own life and putting thought and effort into each exercise—this will allow you to reap the most rewarding benefits. I say this because over the years I've encountered numerous women in individual therapy and workshops, who, with a dedicated effort, have significantly improved their self-esteem and ultimately discovered the path to more happiness and a more fulfilling future. This program can help you, too, develop and improve self-esteem, which will ultimately lead to a more confident, happier, and fulfilling life. Come join me on this journey—you truly deserve it.

PART ONE

THE FOUNDATION

THE ROOTS OF SELF-ESTEEM are established early in life; however, our self-esteem is not necessarily consistent over time. Both internal and external factors affect and shape our self-esteem every day. Our levels of self-esteem can change throughout our life based on different experiences that impact the way we view and value ourselves. Relationships, circumstances, and life events can impact self-esteem, either negatively or positively. The goal for each individual is to develop a solid foundation of healthy self-esteem that remains intact despite (and even because of) life's hardships, struggles, and curveballs. Our struggles are life's tattoos—but they can make us tough and resilient. When we have strong, stable self-esteem, we approach life, relationships, and responsibilities with confidence and optimism.

We'll begin by identifying what self-esteem is, and what it is not. We will talk about the differences between self-esteem and things like confidence and arrogance. We'll also explore why healthy self-esteem is so vital and take a look at some individual cases that highlight the problems that come with having low self-esteem, along with the many benefits of improving self-esteem. Through the exercises in this section, you will begin to identify your own level of self-esteem. This is the beginning of the process—developing greater awareness of the impact your self-esteem has on your life.

CHAPTER 1

What Is Self-Esteem?

SELF-ESTEEM REFERS TO THE IMAGE we have of ourselves in regard to how much value we place on our lives. And developing self-esteem is about respecting ourselves, believing in our own worth, and building the capacity to feel "good enough" just as we are, regardless of what happens in our lives. Self-esteem plays a big role in determining how we will navigate life's challenges—it allows us to either feel happy and fulfilled or sad and empty across the different situations in our lives. Self-esteem isn't about being perfect or about having the approval of others around us. **Rather, it's about accepting yourself the way you are and maintaining an intrinsic belief that you are a good and worthy person simply because you exist as a human.**

Intrinsic self-worth can be a tricky concept to wrap your brain around. It may be something you've never really considered; it might tap into personal and existential belief systems, or it may seem plain foreign due to years of struggles with poor self-esteem. Rather than debate the basis or validity of internal worth, I invite you to step back from any doubt or blocking beliefs that prohibit you from accepting your own sense of self-worth. Think of how you might view a new baby, a child, or a close friend. Chances are, you would easily be able to see their value, yet when self-esteem is low, it may be difficult for you to believe *you* possess that same level of fundamental worth.

When our self-esteem is low, we develop a tendency to measure ourselves with more severe standards than we do with the rest of the world. As you work through this book, challenge yourself to let go of any resistance and simply trust that you, too, have inherent worth. When you put aside your reservations, you will be better able to commit to utilizing the recommended steps and tools to build self-esteem. As your self-esteem begins to improve, you will find the veil that prevented you from believing in your own worth has lifted.

MOLLY'S STORY

Molly came to see me after she was released from the hospital following a suicide attempt. She was a smart, beautiful, and talented high school senior with lots of friends and a bright future. Her caring family was shocked to realize she was struggling with feelings of depression and anxiety so severe that she wanted to end her life.

I immediately liked Molly. She was sweet, funny, and, from my eyes, had so much going for her. She had a family that was incredibly supportive, friends who clearly adored her, and plans to go off to college the following fall. Her main problem was that she was completely unable to see any positives in herself, resulting in such poor self-esteem that she didn't think her life was worth living.

It quickly became clear that Molly's standards for herself were quite unrealistic. While she was kind, forgiving, and fair in her expectations and interactions with her many friends and family members, she constantly beat herself up for even the most minor matters. Internally, she judged herself for everything. Literally every move she made was matched with internal criticism, questioning whether she had said or done something stupid, and hating herself for not being absolutely perfect in every endeavor.

Throughout our work together, we began referencing her "different measuring stick"—the one she used to measure herself but that would not make sense for anyone else. When she'd beat herself up for what she saw as "yet another failure," I'd ask her if she'd judge her best friend, sister, or even a stranger in the same manner. Molly began to see the havoc her unfair and faulty ruler was creating in her life. In time, she was able to interrupt her self-critiques with the image of the faulty ruler. Eventually, she began to consider that imperfection wasn't the end of the world, and just maybe, her life did matter.

Developing and maintaining healthy self-esteem is a process that can take time, yet it is such a worthwhile endeavor for us all. Imagine how much easier life can be when we simply love and accept ourselves as we are. We can all stand to benefit from building self-esteem in some way. Both men and women can utilize the tools helpful in boosting self-esteem. However, there are some unique challenges that women face in navigating the nuances of establishing a foundation of self-worth. In the following sections, we will explore some factors that play a role in women's self-esteem and learn how to overcome these challenges and take charge of life with confidence and improved self-esteem.

There are many definitions of self-esteem and related concepts; however, the following definition is crafted especially for women. I encourage you to keep it in mind as you work through the material in the book:

> Healthy self-esteem is about holding a positive, realistic, and consistent image of yourself that demonstrates self-respect, a sense of unwavering self-worth, and an acceptance that you deserve happiness and fulfillment despite life's imperfections, stereotypes, challenges, and setbacks.

Just like in Molly's story (page 4), self-esteem issues can be difficult to readily identify, as they often go hand in hand with other struggles, like depression, anxiety, and anger issues. Low self-esteem can also be masked by substance use or addiction, or even hidden beneath fabricated displays of self-assurance and happiness. The following story encapsulates the experience of a woman who came to therapy for issues of depression and anger management, but at the root, she was dealing with very low self-esteem. As you read her story, ask yourself this: Could the more obvious struggles in my life involve a broader issue of low self-esteem? The exercises throughout this chapter will also help you determine how low self-esteem may play a role in your life.

DANA'S STORY

Dana came to therapy to address feelings of depression following a recent breakup. She talked about the hurt she experienced when her ex, Ethan, stated he no longer wanted to be friends, and she reported finding it difficult to hold back her anger. She lashed out at him via angry text messages in trying to figure out exactly where things went wrong and caused a scene when she ran into him in public.

Dana reported it was difficult to get out of bed each morning, due to depression over the loss of the relationship and her extreme feelings of shame regarding how she was acting in the wake of the breakup. Dana isolated herself from her friends, embarrassed to let them see her so distraught. To them, she had always been confident and strong-willed, able to speak her mind and stand up for herself.

Dana reminisced about the relationship, explaining that things had been great when the two spent time together, but recalled how she frequently found herself becoming upset and clingy when Ethan didn't make time for her. She understood he sometimes had other commitments, but couldn't help but take it personally. She began telling herself that something must be wrong with her if she wasn't always his priority. She regretted all the nasty and accusatory things she would say to him but admitted she could not control her feelings of rage.

On the surface, Dana's issues seemed to point to grief, depression, and difficulties managing anger, but when we began exploring her feelings more in depth, we realized that very low self-esteem was contributing to her struggles. Her feelings of insecurity caused her to lack confidence in her relationships and constantly feel on edge. Slowly, Dana's goals shifted from trying to win back Ethan to exploring how her low self-esteem contributed to the instability in that relationship and to problems in other areas of her life.

We talked about where Dana's feelings of insecurity and fear of abandonment stemmed from. She learned techniques to counter the years of self-doubt and began implementing tools to improve self-esteem. As a result of her efforts, Dana found herself feeling happier and more confident, and has set herself up to experience more stability in future relationships.

Can you identify any struggles in your life that may relate to problems with self-esteem?

Growing up with half cibling who made fun of me
Living in a country that represses women
Being chubby as a kid & being put on a diet &
Punished when not doing well in school   made fun
of

Self-esteem is not a fixed entity. Your level of self-esteem can change throughout your life and may appear different with different experiences, with different groups of people, and in different situations. It is helpful to view self-esteem on a continuum, with low, negative, or unhealthy self-esteem on one end and high, positive, or healthy self-esteem on the other. The goal is to establish a foundation of healthy self-esteem that is consistent, steady, and unwavering across all areas of your life, even with the most challenging situations life throws your way.

Establishing Your Baseline Self-Esteem

Before you begin to work on improving your self-esteem, it's important to establish your baseline levels of self-esteem across different areas of your life. Make a list in the space provided of the five most important components—groups or settings—that make up your day-to-day experiences, including roles you play or groups of people you interact with. For example, common components might include family, friends, and coworkers; job, school, and home life; and hobbies, activities, clubs, teams, communities, or organizations in which you participate.

Main components in my life:

1. *Meetings at work*
2. *Sending emails at work*
3. *Problem solving at work*
4. *Dating*
5. *Talking to friends*

For each component on your list, consider the following questions:

1. **I feel comfortable when I am in this group or setting.**

   Component 1: _____ Never   _____ Sometimes   _____ Always
   Component 2: _____ Never   _____ Sometimes   _____ Always
   Component 3: _____ Never   _____ Sometimes   _____ Always
   Component 4: _____ Never   _____ Sometimes   _____ Always
   Component 5: _____ Never   _____ Sometimes   _____ Always

2. **I like myself when I am in this group or setting.**

   Component 1: _____ Never   _____ Sometimes   _____ Always
   Component 2: _____ Never   _____ Sometimes   _____ Always
   Component 3: _____ Never   _____ Sometimes   _____ Always
   Component 4: _____ Never   _____ Sometimes   _____ Always
   Component 5: _____ Never   _____ Sometimes   _____ Always

3. **I feel confident when I am in this group or setting.**

   Component 1: _____ Never   _____ Sometimes   _____ Always
   Component 2: _____ Never   _____ Sometimes   _____ Always
   Component 3: _____ Never   _____ Sometimes   _____ Always
   Component 4: _____ Never   _____ Sometimes   _____ Always
   Component 5: _____ Never   _____ Sometimes   _____ Always

4. **I am able to speak my mind freely in this group or setting.**

   Component 1: _____ Never   _____ Sometimes   _____ Always
   Component 2: _____ Never   _____ Sometimes   _____ Always
   Component 3: _____ Never   _____ Sometimes   _____ Always
   Component 4: _____ Never   _____ Sometimes   _____ Always
   Component 5: _____ Never   _____ Sometimes   _____ Always

5. **I feel valued in this group or setting.**

Component 1:	_____ Never	_____ Sometimes	_____ Always
Component 2:	_____ Never	_____ Sometimes	_____ Always
Component 3:	_____ Never	_____ Sometimes	_____ Always
Component 4:	_____ Never	_____ Sometimes	_____ Always
Component 5:	_____ Never	_____ Sometimes	_____ Always

Now, add up your scores indicating how many times you selected "never," "sometimes," and "always" for each item.

Component 1:	_0_ Never	_5_ Sometimes	_0_ Always
Component 2:	_0_ Never	_5_ Sometimes	_0_ Always
Component 3:	_0_ Never	_5_ Sometimes	_0_ Always
Component 4:	_0_ Never	_5_ Sometimes	_0_ Always
Component 5:	_0_ Never	_5_ Sometimes	_0_ Always

If you checked "never" more than "always," your self-esteem is likely low for this component, whereas if you checked "always" more than "never," your self-esteem is likely higher for this component. If you scored mostly "sometimes" or if your scores are more even, your self-esteem is likely somewhere in the middle. For each of the five components you identified, mark where you believe you fall on the self-esteem continuum provided. Look at the five marks. Judging from where you placed them, where does your overall level of self-esteem seem to rest?

SELF-ESTEEM CONTINUUM

Low ▓▓▓▓▓▓▓▓▓▓▓▓▓▓▓▓▓▓▓▓▓▓▓▓ High

As you work through this book, keep an eye out for the areas of your life where your self-esteem may be falling lower on the continuum. For some people, this can mean nearly all areas, while for others, it may be one or two particularly challenging aspects. Remember, the goal is to improve self-esteem so that it is consistently high across all components of your life.

ASSESSING YOUR SELF-ESTEEM

Write a few sentences about why you think your self-esteem falls where it does for each item you marked on the continuum. Can you identify any obstacles that hold you back from having more self-esteem for the components you marked on the lower end of the scale? What prevents you from feeling a greater sense of self-worth in this area? If you marked anything on the higher end of the scale, what qualities, traits, or circumstances allow for a higher score?

Component 1: Meeting at work

If I am knowledgeable I feel confident
if not I don't

Component 2: Sending email

same as above

Component 3: Problem same as abow

same as abow

Component 4: *Dating*

if I don't care about the person I feel confident to be me

Component 5: *Tally + friend*

when I know the person I feel I can be myself

Healthy Self-Esteem

We know what self-esteem is and identified where ours generally falls on the continuum. We recognize that healthy self-esteem across all areas of life is the goal. Now let's talk about what healthy self-esteem looks like.

Generally speaking, women with healthy self-esteem see themselves as worthwhile and capable. They have an accurate view of themselves and feel secure, even while facing challenges or setbacks. They are able to recognize and appreciate their strengths, and also accept their shortcomings, realizing that flaws and weaknesses are an inevitable part of life. Women with healthy self-esteem set healthy goals and feel deserving and capable of good. They respect themselves and engage in healthy behaviors.

Healthy self-esteem comes with an understanding that your value is not determined by perfection or accomplishments, and that worth does not have to be proven or earned. Rather, self-worth is a given. It comes from within, from a deep personal belief that you are fundamentally good. It does not involve getting caught up in seeking worth through external sources or gaining reassurance through the approval, validation, or attention of others.

THE BENEFITS OF HEALTHY SELF-ESTEEM

Even if it takes some work to get there, healthy self-esteem is a gift that we can give ourselves, with many rewards.

Women with healthy self-esteem **tend to have balance in their lives**. This is because they:

· Feel a sense of purpose
· Recognize their own efforts
· Take pride in their accomplishments
· Give themselves credit where credit is due
· Trust their gut and follow their instincts
· Feel confident in their own opinions
· Make choices and act without constantly second-guessing themselves
· Avoid getting entangled in self-doubt
· Avoid preoccupation with the need to be perfect
· Avoid worrying about what others think

Women with healthy self-esteem **enjoy a realistic and authentic sense of self**. This is because they:

· Take responsibility for their own actions
· Don't engage in unnecessary self-blame or self-deprecating thinking
· Accept mistakes with grace and learn from them, understanding that mistakes are inevitable
· Do not unjustly blame or project their shortcomings on others
· Avoid engaging in unwarranted and persistent apologizing

Women with healthy self-esteem **enjoy a healthy balance of independence and interdependence**. This is because they:

· Are self-sufficient
· Think for themselves
· Avoid excessively comparing themselves to others
· Make their own decisions without fear of judgment by others

- Can enjoy time alone without anxiety or fear of abandonment
- Are not needy, clingy, or insecure in relationships

Women with healthy self-esteem **enjoy strong and healthy relationships**. This is because they:

- Value and expect honesty, trust, and equality
- Set appropriate limits and establish clear boundaries with others
- Communicate effectively to resolve problems
- Act assertively
- Ask for help when necessary without guilt, trepidation, or feelings of being a burden
- Set realistic standards and goals for themselves and others
- Live according to their own values and principles
- Don't let others sway their decisions
- Don't fall prey to peer pressure or manipulation

Women with healthy self-esteem **are better equipped to deal with stress**. This is because they:

- Can self-soothe
- Can manage their lives
- Do not constantly look externally for reassurance, guidance, and validation
- Approach problems rationally and sensibly
- Know how to walk away from toxic people and harmful environments

ANNA'S STORY

When Anna first started therapy, she talked about feeling depressed. She had dropped out of college, was fired from a job due to too many absences, and found herself feeling completely lost. She was frustrated that members of her family treated her as if she was broken, so she avoided them, spending a lot of time at her boyfriend's house instead.

The more I got to know Anna, the more I recognized just how low her self-esteem was. Her lack of self-worth contributed to a number of struggles in her past, including difficulty committing to school and work, constant drama at home and with friends, and a history of harmful actions, including promis-cuity, excessive drinking, and cutting.

I encouraged Anna to sign up for one of my self-esteem workshops. She initially felt hesitant, but agreed. Being among a group of women who experi-enced similar feelings of self-doubt helped her feel less alone. She found great benefit in the material she learned, and she started to consider that maybe it was possible for her to get her life back on track. Feeling less discouraged, she worked to stop seeing herself as damaged and to instead begin nurturing herself and believing that her life has potential. Over the next year, Anna worked incredibly hard to build her self-esteem. She followed all of the recommended steps and tools I gave her and began making positive changes in her life.

She eventually realized her boyfriend did not respect her and decided being single for a while might not be so bad. She enrolled in a class at the com-munity college and began considering a future career in business. She found a new part-time job, where she was able to put her tools into practice, taking responsibility for her own actions and implementing assertiveness skills in communicating with coworkers and managers.

It wasn't an overnight change, but in time, Anna began to respect her-self more. In developing her own sense of self-esteem, Anna was able to get her life back on track, experience healthier relationships, and move forward toward her goals.

SELF-ESTEEM CHECKLIST

Take a look at the following two lists. The first list contains statements that encompass the characteristics and belief systems reflecting healthy self-esteem. The second list includes problems and patterns associated with low self-esteem. Check off any items that you identify with on both lists.

Give yourself credit for any checks you make on the healthy-self-esteem list. Use the checks on the low-self-esteem list to identify areas you'll want to pay special attention to as you work through this book. While you're at it, highlight the items from the healthy-self-esteem list that you are especially hoping to develop.

Healthy Self-Esteem

- ☐ I am worthy ✓
- ☑ I am capable
- ☐ I can handle challenges and setbacks ✓
- ☐ I take pride in my strengths and accomplishments
- ☐ I can accept my weaknesses ✓
- ☐ I am okay with imperfection ✓
- ☑ I accept and learn from mistakes
- ☐ I don't need to prove myself to anyone ✓
- ☑ I am proud of my efforts
- ☑ I take responsibility for my own actions
- ☐ I am able to make decisions ✓
- ☐ I am able to stand up for and protect myself ✓
- ☑ I sometimes enjoy being alone
- ☐ I am comfortable in group settings ✓
- ☑ I am able to think for myself
- ☑ I am able to ask for help when necessary
- ☐ I am able to accept compliments
- ☐ I am able to handle criticism
- ☐ I don't fixate on the judgments of others ✓
- ☐ My relationships are generally healthy and fulfilling
- ☐ I am able to set limits and boundaries ✓
- ☑ I am able to effectively communicate with others
- ☐ I have realistic expectations and standards
- ☐ I am happy with my values and principles
- ☐ I am able to handle stress ✓
- ☑ I am able to self-soothe
- ☐ I am able to handle disappointment or grief
- ☐ My life has meaning and purpose ✓

Low Self-Esteem

- ☑ I spend a lot of time worried about what others think
- ☑ I frequently doubt myself
- ☐ I often feel a sense of shame

- ☑ I am indecisive and find it hard to trust my own judgments
- ☑ I tend to put things off or delay starting tasks and projects
- ☐ I tend to blame others when things don't work out
- ☐ I often feel like a victim
- ☑ I often feel anxious or depressed
- ☐ I often feel guilty
- ☑ I feel a need to be perfect
- ☑ I often find myself apologizing
- ☑ I often feel like a burden
- ☐ I have difficulty relying on others or asking for help
- ☑ I find it uncomfortable to make eye contact
- ☑ I believe other people's thoughts and opinions are more important than mine
- ☑ I often feel taken advantage of by others
- ☐ I find it difficult to end toxic or abusive relationships
- ☑ I easily succumb to peer pressure
- ☐ I rely on others to make me feel good
- ☑ I frequently seek approval from others
- ☑ I crave reassurance and compliments
- ☑ I find it very difficult when others are mad or upset with me
- ☐ I have difficulty hearing criticism, whether constructive or otherwise
- ☑ I feel uncomfortable when people compliment or praise me
- ☑ I frequently compare myself to others
- ☐ I find it hard to speak up for myself
- ☑ I have trouble managing stress
- ☑ I often become overwhelmed

WHAT SELF-ESTEEM IS NOT

Healthy self-esteem is not about being perfect or flawless; rather, it's about accepting yourself as you are and being realistic with your own expectations. Stop and consider this: you already are a worthy person, regardless of the things you have or have not done. The key to self-esteem is simply in believing it. People with healthy self-esteem aren't perfect. They know they have weaknesses, but they accept themselves as they are. Healthy self-esteem involves

BELIEVING IN YOUR SELF-ESTEEM RIGHTS

As humans, we all have certain basic rights; however, these rights are not always obvious. You might not have learned these rights in childhood, or you may have forgotten them over the years. Building self-esteem involves developing awareness of, internalizing, and believing in the following principles.

As you read over the list, note the points that feel particularly foreign or difficult to accept. The items that you find the hardest to believe indicate areas where you will likely need to focus the most attention and do the most work.

10 PRINCIPLES OF HEALTHY SELF-ESTEEM

1. I know I have infinite, inherent, and unconditional worth simply because I am human.

2. I have the right to be imperfect, to make mistakes, and to accept my flaws and weaknesses.

3. I have the freedom to establish my own beliefs, values, and standards, and to accept that they may differ from those of others.

4. I give myself permission to ask for what I want, to expect the best for myself, and to experience disappointment when my needs are not met.

5. I am able to respectfully express my needs, opinions, and desires without fearing the reaction of others.

6. I am entitled to make my own decisions, and I have the right to change my mind.

7. I have the right to protect myself and to say no to things that are not in my best interest.

8. I deserve respect from others and have the right to establish boundaries that ensure my well-being.

9. I have the right to change, grow, and be emotionally healthy, regardless of my past or the conditions of those around me.

10. I know, care for, respect, accept, and love myself unconditionally.

acknowledging that we all have strengths and weaknesses and entails the recognition that flaws are both inevitable and irrelevant to worth. It's not about hiding imperfections, being inauthentic, or boasting about successes. Healthy self-esteem does not involve conforming to the wishes and demands of others, nor does it depend on anyone else's approval in order to feel okay. It's about trusting in oneself.

Self-esteem is different from confidence in that self-esteem refers to how you feel about your total core self overall. It is the all-encompassing assessment you make regarding your entire existence. Confidence, on the other hand, relates to your level of self-assurance in regard to specific traits, abilities, or encounters. Confidence is about trusting in your ability to be successful or perform well in a specific endeavor or during a moment in time. Confidence will inevitably vary based on our individual skills, talents, and gifts, and lacking confidence in a particular area is not necessarily a bad thing. We all have strengths and weaknesses and, logically, we cannot be good at everything. The goal is to have healthy, intact self-esteem, even when confidence may be low.

For example, if you know you are not great at a certain thing, say ice-skating, your confidence in your ability to gracefully coast across the ice and perform triple axels will undoubtedly be quite low. With self-esteem, the question is, how does knowing you aren't a great skater or the experience of falling on the ice make you feel about yourself? If you beat yourself up for not being better or find yourself equating your skating ability with your self-worth, your self-esteem will be low, creating problems with mood, motivation, and your overall ability to feel good enough. With healthy self-esteem, the recognition that you are a valuable and worthy person prevails despite your weak skating abilities.

Self-esteem is also very different from arrogance and narcissism. Arrogant and narcissistic people may appear to hold themselves in great regard due to their self-absorbed disposition; however, their selfishness and egotistical nature are often a front for low self-esteem. The self-centered mind-set and actions of narcissists are typically ineffective attempts at gaining self-worth. People who bully, or are arrogant or narcissistic, act selfishly and as if they are superior, putting others down in the process. They make decisions and actions without regard for others, failing to consider the feelings or positions of anyone else.

This can be particularly damaging if the other person has low self-esteem, as they might take it as "proof" that they are not worthy instead of accepting that the problem lies with the offender.

Self-esteem, on the other hand, involves maintaining respect for everyone. With healthy self-esteem, you respect yourself, generally feel good about yourself, and are able to take pride in your accomplishments, but you also demonstrate respect and appreciation for others around you. You acknowledge that everyone has inherent worth, and you value different thoughts, opinions, and feelings. You do not seek to build yourself up at the expense of anyone else.

JILL'S STORY

When Jill first began talking about her difficulties in dating, I was struck by her level of what seemed like arrogance. She talked about immediately rejecting men who did not meet her strict criteria and rattled off a list of the dates she'd been on since we'd last met, along with the reasons a second date was not in the cards.

The first guy was too short, and she'd never be able to wear heels. The second one had an unimpressive job. The third one bored her to tears with talk about his hobbies. The fourth one was okay but nothing special. And then there were all the others she didn't even consider going out with, due to either a lack of attraction to their pictures or irritation with something they had written in their online profiles.

I couldn't help but recognize how superficial and unrealistic Jill seemed in regard to the expectations she had for her love life. But as we began to dig deeper, it became clear that Jill's hypercritical attitude was, in fact, masking her low self-esteem.

The more we talked, the more apparent it became that she was filled with anxiety, self-doubt, and an overwhelming fear of rejection. She lacked confidence in her ability to make a good impression on dates, so she subconsciously created a pattern of rejecting people before they had a chance to reject her. Being rejected would confirm her conviction that she was not worthy. Yet, she still continued to search for the ideal man, falsely believing that a relationship was what she needed in order to feel whole. It became a vicious cycle, leaving her feeling frustrated and deflated.

The problem was that Jill was searching for external validation and sabotaging potential relationships before they even had a chance to begin. To that end, we talked a lot about what it would be like for Jill to allow herself to be more vulnerable, and what might happen if she could be more honest regarding her dating anxiety. We decided that it was okay for her to simply explain to her dates that she was very nervous—after all, isn't everyone nervous on a first date? In fact, such candor would probably be appreciated. Jill also worked very hard to develop self-compassion and to minimize her habit of constantly belittling herself.

Eventually, Jill began to build self-esteem and allowed herself to let down her guard when it came to dating. She recently began dating a good guy. He's not perfect, of course, and there have been some bumps along the way as she works to overcome her insecurities and stop fearing that things will inevitably not work out; but he adores her, respects her, and challenges her to continue accepting that she is good enough just as she is.

Roots of Self-Esteem

As we've discussed, self-esteem is not always a fixed entity. The roots of self-esteem form early in childhood, but the level of self-esteem you experience can change over time. If you are reading this book, it's probably safe to say that your self-esteem is not in an optimal place. The exercises you've done up to now may have shed some light on your level of self-esteem, or given you some insight into the kinds of individual struggles you may be facing in light of self-esteem issues. As you begin to gain awareness of the significant impact low self-esteem can have, don't be discouraged. Self-esteem is not written in stone, and awareness is an important first step toward achieving your goals.

Moving forward, it will be helpful to understand where your low self-esteem may stem from. Early relationships and experiences form the basis of self-esteem, so it's useful to reflect on what your childhood was like. We'll take a look at early messages you received and think about what you witnessed in role models growing up. Unique circumstances can play a role in a woman's ability to develop and maintain self-esteem. In the next chapter, we will explore some of these factors so you can be prepared to prevent them from getting in your way. Later, in part 2, we will explore more deeply how your own early experiences may have contributed to your self-esteem challenges, before moving on to learn tools and steps for creating positive change.

> If your low self-esteem is a result of any form of abuse, whether physical, emotional, mental, or sexual, please put down this book and find a qualified and experienced therapist to help you heal. The steps in this book will be essential to your recovery and your ability to move forward in a positive direction; however, dealing with the traumatic nature and emotional fallout of the abuse must come first. Developing self-esteem in the aftermath of abuse is a journey you should not travel alone—instead, seek the counsel and guidance of a supportive professional. Please see the Resources section (page 201) at the end of this book for help finding support near you.

INITIAL REFLECTIONS: YOUR STORY AND SELF-ESTEEM

Before we move on, take some time to think about your own life, your current struggles, and your reactions to the information and exercises in this chapter.

How do you currently feel about your level of self-esteem?

I have low self esteem

How might low self-esteem be related to the struggles, stressors, or challenges in your life?

not getting promoted
not being in a relationship
unable to make decisions
anxiety & depression

What experiences from your past have perhaps held you back from having healthier self-esteem?

brother making fun of me, my mom favoring
my brother, being punished due to my dad's action
living in an opressed country, seeing my mom
struggle as a woman

Did anything regarding the description of what self-esteem is (or is not) surprise you?

Yes that it is not the same as confidence

What is your biggest revelation or takeaway from this chapter?

● ● ● ● ●

CHAPTER 2

For Women Only

LOW SELF-ESTEEM CAN BE A PROBLEM for both men and women, but women face challenges unique to their gender. This chapter explores how things like society, culture, and genetic makeup play vital roles in women's self-esteem. It also points to specific factors that can contribute to low self-esteem for women, as well as the barriers women face when trying to boost self-esteem.

Have you ever noticed that, in general, women tend to display lower levels of self-esteem compared to men? For instance, when was the last time you heard a man complain that he was having a bad hair day? Or asking others if his outfit made him look fat? Is it just that women convey their lack of self-esteem more readily? Why do men in our society seem to be more self-assured? Is there really a biological difference between the two genders that lends itself to disparities in self-esteem?

A 2016 study detailed the findings of the first large-scale, cross-cultural investigation of gender and age differences in self-esteem. This study found that, consistent with previous studies conducted in the United States and other Western industrialized countries, at every age, men *do* tend to have higher levels of self-esteem than women worldwide. Women tend to have more equality in our society compared to other parts of the world; however, the gender gap related to self-esteem still exists and actually is larger than in poorer, less developed countries with greater gender inequality. Is it possible that the pursuit of gender equality in our society may be challenging, rather than helping, women in their quest for positive self-esteem?

The Gender Gap in Self-Esteem

The following exercise can help you gauge whether you have witnessed and/or experienced a gender gap regarding self-esteem in your own circles. There are no right or wrong answers—your responses are simply your opinions based on your own relationships, experiences, and current level of self-esteem.

Compared to men, women tend to have a harder time:

1. Feeling confident	TRUE	FALSE
2. Making up their minds	TRUE	FALSE
3. Making decisions	TRUE	FALSE
4. Being assertive	TRUE	FALSE
5. Saying no	TRUE	FALSE
6. Trusting their gut	TRUE	FALSE
7. Expressing their thoughts, opinions, and feelings	TRUE	FALSE
8. Asking for help	TRUE	FALSE
9. Making financial decisions	TRUE	FALSE
10. Accepting criticism	TRUE	FALSE
11. Maintaining composure	TRUE	FALSE
12. Avoiding moodiness	TRUE	FALSE
13. Dealing with anger	TRUE	FALSE
14. Distancing themselves from destructive relationships	TRUE	FALSE

Again, there are not any right or wrong answers. These are general statements. Every man and woman differs in their ability to do these things; however, if you marked any statements as true, you likely do observe and/or experience a gender gap related to self-esteem. It's important to keep in mind how this gender gap may impact how you view yourself. Think about the following questions:

What differences have you observed in regard to the overall self-esteem of men versus women? Think of what you have experienced in your family, among your friends, and in the workplace.

Men don't apologize a lot, They speak their mind in meetings even if they are wrong, they worry less about appearance They don't think that they don't deserve good things

What have you personally experienced in the way you are treated by men? What have you experienced in how you are treated compared to how men are treated?

My voice is heard less, I get interrupted more, not noticed in meeting.

Are there any lessons or messages you have drawn about the world or about yourself in response to your perceptions of a gender gap?

What obstacles and barriers do you believe contribute to the gender gap as it pertains to self-esteem?

_____

_____

_____

_____

Being aware of the gender gap, your perceptions, and the unique challenges that women face can help you in your journey to build strong self-esteem. A difference in the treatment of men and women, in their self-perceptions, and in their ability to maintain self-esteem does in fact exist, and it varies by culture. By recognizing the obstacles women face, you can work to prevent these challenges from holding you back as you build the healthy self-esteem you inherently deserve.

The Way We're Wired

If you have ever been in a relationship or even a deep conversation with a man, you are probably well aware that men and women have some real, innate differences in terms of how they think and interact. Think of the book *Men Are from Mars, Women Are from Venus*. It's a remarkable phenomenon. And research shows that the brains of men and women are, in fact, hardwired differently. Understanding the differences in male and female biology and brain chemistry can help us, in turn, better understand why discrepancies between the genders exist and remove some of the barriers that may prevent women from improving their self-esteem.

In line with findings from the aforementioned gender study (page 23), there is credible evidence that genetics play a role in the development of and capacity for self-esteem. Several studies have shown male traits to be positively correlated with self-esteem and feminine traits to show a weaker and less consistent link with self-esteem. Therefore, it would stand to reason that women face more challenges in terms of building and maintaining self-esteem. Exploring these fundamental and biological differences can shed light on misunderstandings and stressors that tend to chip away at feelings of self-worth.

Imagine that you come home from a particularly terrible day and begin telling your male partner about all the stressors on your plate. He responds by asking you if you've tried *x*, suggesting you do *y*, and recommending *z*. Chances are, your female brain will become infuriated by his lack of validation and his propensity to jump to solve the problem before he's taken any time to truly empathize with your feelings of stress.

When you are stuck in a place of low self-esteem, you may become flooded with thoughts like, *"He doesn't want to be bothered with my issues. He doesn't care about me at all. He thinks I'm weak for not handling the pressure better. I should be better able to handle everything."* These types of thoughts create tension in relationships, keep you stuck feeling bad about yourself, and add to the feeling of being overwhelmed.

Did you know that during stress or pressure, the spatial ability and logic functioning areas of the brain are activated for men, while the speech function is what becomes activated for women? By understanding this, you can gain a more rational perspective on why your partner is responding to the situation in that manner. Instead of making self-berating assumptions, it can help to remind yourself, *"Okay, he's being a man. He has a man brain. I'm a talker, he's a problem-solver."* This way, you can take the situation at face value, avoid relationship conflict, and protect your self-esteem from damage by untrue and self-deprecating thoughts.

BRAIN CHEMISTRY

Differences in brain chemistry and structure affect and contribute to contrasts between the genders in both thinking patterns and behavior. Brain-imaging studies show variances between male and female brains in terms of size and how different regions of the brain function. Studies have shown female brains have more strongly coordinated activity between hemispheres, while the activity of male brains is more tightly coordinated within local brain regions.

In general, women have more finely tuned sensory skills, are more sensitive to touch, are more emotional, and are wired to respond more to people and faces versus objects and shapes. They tend to do better with verbal ability, reading comprehension, writing ability, fine-motor coordination, perceptual speed, and long-term memory. Men, on the other hand, tend to pay less attention to detail, are more direct and literal, and are drawn to things and how they work rather than relationships and communication. They demonstrate superior visuospatial skills and are better at juggling items in their working memory.

Women have specific areas in both sides of the brain that deal with speech and language. This makes them good conversationalists, and it's what drives women's need to talk about and acknowledge problems in order to work them out and get them off their minds. Men, on the other hand, have more highly compartmentalized brains and are better able to separate and store information and emotions. Simply put, male and female brains work differently, but the differences don't mean either gender is better, smarter, or more worthy!

Many of these differences, especially the ones related to knowledge acquisition, appear very early in life. Differences in spatial-visualization ability can be seen in two- and three-month-old infants, and studies with both rhesus monkeys and human babies have shown marked differences between genders regarding preference in toys, with males preferring stereotypically "boy toys"—those with wheels—while females preferred plush toys. For decades, research has demonstrated the existence of innate gender differences; however, researchers are still working to understand exactly how our gender and brains impact feelings of self-worth. A 2014 Dartmouth College study suggests that the way different regions of the brain connect and integrate information may work differently for men and women, thus playing a biological role in the self-esteem gap experienced across the genders.

HORMONES

Hormones, namely estrogen, progesterone, and testosterone, also play a role in the biological differences between men and women. These hormones affect the brain and, therefore, impact mood and behavior. Men's hormones stay relatively stable, while women's hormones fluctuate over a roughly 28-day cycle to support reproductive functioning. This results in shifts in mood and changes in the fat-to-protein ratio in our bodies, in order to support pregnancy and breastfeeding.

For women, the loss of progesterone coupled with low levels of estrogen before menstruation can contribute to several changes in mood and behavior. Estrogen is a precursor to the neurotransmitter serotonin, the chemical in the brain responsible for balancing mood and preventing depression. When hormones shift during the menstrual cycle, so do neurotransmitters, causing many women to feel depressed, anxious, frustrated, or just plain "off." Research shows that it's the shifts in hormones that cause the most trouble with mental functioning. Therefore, women—who experience menstruation, pregnancy, postpartum periods, and menopause—are more affected than men.

Studies show that unbalanced levels of certain hormones can lead to symptoms of depression and anxiety. To date, however, only a few studies have examined hormonal influences regarding gender differences and self-esteem. One study did find that the timing of puberty influences body image and self-esteem, which makes sense. Adolescence can be a challenging time for girls, particularly when it comes to maintaining self-esteem. The tendency to compare ourselves to peers in regard to appearance and maturity affects how we view ourselves.

Adolescent Pressures

Think back to your own adolescent years and reflect on the pressures and changes that may have impacted your self-esteem. What do you remember experiencing?

I was called fat, I wanted to be skinny like other girls

Tracking Cycles

Hormones greatly contribute to our moods and the way we feel about ourselves at various times throughout life and over the course of each monthly cycle. Over the next few months, pay attention to times you experience any of the following symptoms, and track them on the following calendars.

Potential symptoms related to hormones can include:

- Depression
- Increased irritability
- Increased sensitivity
- Feeling useless
- Restlessness
- Exhaustion
- Increased energy

- Heightened attention
- Difficulty concentrating
- Feeling bloated
- Poor body image
- Increased or decreased sex drive
- Feeling not at all like yourself

MONTH _____

SUN	MON	TUE	WED	THU	FRI	SAT

MONTH _____

SUN	MON	TUE	WED	THU	FRI	SAT

MONTH _____

SUN	MON	TUE	WED	THU	FRI	SAT

As you begin tracking, see if you notice any patterns that you might be able to attribute to your hormones. When you become more aware of how and when hormones are to blame for changes in mood and behavior, you can prevent these resulting emotions from taking a toll on your self-esteem. How? Rather than beat yourself up for any of these symptoms, simply recognize it's not your fault, know that it's temporary, and move on.

NATALIE'S STORY

I began seeing Natalie when she was a freshman in high school. We worked together for several years, until she went off to college. During our work together, Natalie talked about social anxiety and low self-esteem, stress related to her parents' divorce, and the pressures of high school. I was always impressed with how wise and self-aware Natalie was for her age. After she had made quite a bit of progress and was functioning well overall, we tapered her sessions to every other week. Natalie was in a good place but chose to continue regular therapy, recognizing she benefited from having a place to check in.

Toward the end of Natalie's junior year, I noticed her moods became more unpredictable. She arrived at some sessions upbeat and excited to tell me about the latest updates in her life, but came to others seeming cranky and irritable. Her symptoms of anxiety and feelings of low self-esteem seemed to be returning.

Over the next several months, I started to note a pattern in Natalie's presentation and questioned whether her highs and lows might be related to her menstrual cycle. Together we began tracking how she was feeling and determined that her period did contribute to the increase in anxiety. Normally, she felt confident in her social circle and breezed through school as an exemplary student. But during her time of the month, she overanalyzed everything she said and did, questioned whether her friends really liked her, and became increasingly stressed about tests and schoolwork.

I began pointing out this tendency to Natalie. When she was feeling anxious and overwhelmed, I reminded her, "This happened last month, remember? But it won't last forever." It was initially difficult for her to identify the shifts in her mood on her own and to recognize them as being temporary or related to a pattern. Being reminded that her negative feelings were likely symptoms of her hormones helped her to accept what was happening, instead of getting worked up with fear that she was losing control. Rather than put her energy into beating herself up for setbacks, she began focusing on tools she could implement to weather the storm.

The Life Cycle

As we've learned, self-esteem can ebb and flow throughout various phases of a woman's life. Similarly, hormones can shift regularly for women, creating drastic changes at different periods and stages. A greater understanding of the various changes women face can help mitigate negative impacts to self-esteem. Conversely, this knowledge can empower women to recognize our toughness— we weather many ups and downs just by the nature of our gender and our physiological makeup!

The 2016 study (page 23) noting the worldwide gender gap showed that the gap emerges in adolescence and persists throughout early and middle adulthood before it narrows and perhaps even disappears with old age. Following is a look at different stages in a woman's life, along with factors that tend to influence a woman's self-esteem. As you read through the stages, note which experiences you have personally encountered or witnessed in others, and consider how these stages might have impacted your self-esteem.

INFANCY

Children are born carefree, and newborns and babies haven't yet learned to individuate themselves from others. Their interaction with caretakers begins to lay the groundwork for self-esteem. Knowing that they are loved and well cared for helps babies create a foundation of healthy self-esteem.

Notes and experiences:

_____

_____

_____

_____

TODDLER YEARS

Toddlers begin to gain a sense of identity by exploring the world and learning what they can do. They look to others around them for reassurance, and they begin internalizing messages about who they are from their interactions with others. The development of toddlers' self-esteem is also influenced by what they witness in their role models.

Notes and experiences:

_____

_____

_____

_____

PRESCHOOL YEARS

During the preschool years, children have a better understanding that they are unique individuals. They begin making comparisons of themselves to others and begin recognizing the differences between males and females. Preschoolers begin facing experiences that can either build up their self-esteem or tear it down.

Notes and experiences:

_____

_____

_____

_____

ELEMENTARY YEARS

Older children continue to receive messages that they internalize as they are developing their sense of identity. They have more social interactions, and everything they personally experience or witness in others plays a role in forming their levels of self-esteem.

Notes and experiences:

_____

_____

_____

_____

ADOLESCENCE

By adolescence, individuals have an established self-image and have formed habits that dictate their fundamental levels of self-esteem. During this time, the body and brain are maturing and going through puberty. The many biological changes, new experiences, and additional pressures of the teen years create extra challenges to maintaining healthy self-esteem.

Notes and experiences:

_____

_____

_____

_____

YOUNG ADULTHOOD

Young adulthood is a time when individuals develop new relationships, take on adult roles, and expand their horizons as they realize their independence. These experiences continue to impact levels of self-esteem, positively, negatively, or both.

Notes and experiences:

_____

_____

_____

_____

MIDDLE AGE

Middle age can be an empowering time for some and a challenging time for others in terms of maintaining healthy self-esteem. Because our society is so focused on maintaining youth and beauty, some women face aging with stress, fear, and regrets. Physical changes, such as weight gain, wrinkles, and graying hair, can take a toll on body image and negatively impact self-esteem.

Notes and experiences:

_____

_____

_____

_____

PERIMENOPAUSE

Peri- or pre-menopause typically happens during a woman's 40s or 50s, but can occur earlier or later in some cases. During this time, a woman's hormone production begins to fluctuate and estrogen declines, which can cause a wide range of symptoms, both physical and emotional, that can play a role in self-esteem.

Notes and experiences:

_____

_____

_____

_____

MENOPAUSE

Menopause can be a wonderful stage for women who, after all the ups and downs, simply feel comfortable in their own skin, but this stage also brings about a number of transitions that can create increased feelings of uncertainty and vulnerability. The decrease in estrogen that occurs in menopause leads to low levels of the enzyme monoamine oxidase, which damages and destroys neuro-transmitters, including dopamine, serotonin, and norepinephrine. These chemicals regulate things like moods and behaviors. Changes in these areas, along with facing aging, the passing of childbearing years, and increasing physical symp-toms that accompany aging, can pose a real threat to self-confidence and self-esteem for women.

Notes and experiences:

_____

_____

_____

_____

OLDER AGE

Self-esteem can sometimes increase in older age, when post-menopausal women accept and even embrace aging and come to terms with physical and emotional changes. However, women also tend to live longer than men, and often their additional years are spent navigating illnesses and disabilities, which can negatively impact self-image. Women are more likely than men to be widowed, and this change can lead to feelings of loneliness that can also play a role in self-esteem.

Notes and experiences:

_____

_____

_____

_____

Motherhood . . . or Not

Pregnancy and childbirth bring about some of the greatest changes in hormones; thus, women who become mothers can face additional challenges in maintaining healthy self-esteem. Research has found that women tend to experience declines in self-esteem during pregnancies. Of course, this does not happen to everyone—some pregnant women feel unstoppable. While it may rise again during the six months after delivery, self-esteem is shown to continue to decrease during the early years of parenting, showing lower levels at three years postpartum than at the original baseline. These findings can be attributed to physical changes to a woman's body, fluctuations in hormones, and the stress and uncertainties that accompany parenting.

Additionally, studies have found that women's estimation of their romantic relationship tends to fall drastically after having a child. Women who report a decrease in relationship satisfaction also report lower self-esteem. A troubled relationship and lower self-esteem tend to go hand in hand, and the advent of parenthood can exacerbate both.

It should be stated that motherhood can be a most joyous and empowering experience. But balancing motherhood with other aspects of a woman's identity can prove a challenge that tests women's ability to maintain healthy self-esteem. For example, most mothers take at least a period of time off for maternity leave, and some stay home for several years to raise their children before returning to the workforce. Lack of confidence and low self-esteem are cited as the most significant challenges women face when returning to work. Mothers who choose to give up careers to stay home indefinitely can love it; but some experience diminished self-esteem due to a loss of identity and a perceived or real loss of bargaining power as an outright financial contributor. Envy over friends who get to put on work clothes and maintain their roles in a "grown-up" environment can also impact self-esteem.

BECOMING A MOM

If you are a mother, think about how pregnancy, childbirth, and parenting have impacted your levels of self-esteem, either negatively or positively. What have you noticed about your own self-esteem with regard to becoming and being a mom?

_____

_____

_____

_____

What changes have you experienced regarding your relationships with your partner, family, and friends as a result of becoming a mother? How have these changes impacted your self-esteem?

_____

_____

_____

_____

Make a list of pros and cons as they relate to your work-life balance as a mother. (Remember, there is no such thing as a nonworking mother—even if you are a stay-at-home mom, make sure you include household and parenting duties in your list.)

PROS	CONS

What parts do you find satisfying? Which parts are unsatisfying? Is there a balance; if not, what needs more attention?

NOT BEING A MOM

The experience of *not* being a mother can also affect self-esteem. Some women choose not to have children, and others who desperately wish to become a mom may not get the opportunity due to infertility, absence of a willing partner, lack of resources, or other issues that get in the way of bearing children. If you have reached the stage in your life where you want or wanted to become a mom but aren't fulfilling that goal, or if you have intentionally chosen not to become a mother, think about how not being a mom has influenced your self-esteem. How has this experience impacted your view of yourself? Has it strengthened or empowered you, or has it taken an emotional toll? How have your relationships changed or been affected as a result?

I wonder if I'll be less of a woman if I don't have kids or if I'll be missing out on life

Many Variables on the Path to Self-Esteem

When we think about all the different variables a woman faces, it may seem like we drew the short stick when it comes to biology and striving to build healthy self-esteem! However, please don't let these biological differences scare you into believing it's impossible for women to have healthy self-esteem. Regardless of any influence that may impact self-esteem (age, personality, life circumstances, etc.), your level of self-esteem is *not* set in stone. No matter where your self-esteem currently lies, you *can* improve it.

Research shows that our brains are constantly changing and adapting with every experience in our lives. New brain cells are constantly being created, which means we have the power to literally rewire our brains through our actions. The steps in the following section of this book will show you how to do this. By 1) identifying the habits that have trapped you in a place of low self-esteem, and 2) implementing new tools and creating healthier habits, you can actually change your brain patterns and improve your own level of self-esteem.

Before we move on to these tools, let's first look at a few other challenges that women face. Successfully working through this program involves developing a keener awareness of external obstacles and barriers in our society that can come into play as you move through the steps in part 2.

External Expectations
(and Their Influences)

One of the biggest challenges for women in terms of building self-esteem is navigating the constant barrage of expectations and stereotypes conveyed by our society and various people in our lives. In our culture, differences between males and females can be observed early on, as children are routinely socialized according to gender from birth. Different norms for boys and girls are demonstrated through colors, toys, and clothing chosen for boys versus girls, often before a child is even born. Also, separate traits and characteristics are valued in different genders. For example, boys are often expected and encouraged to be tough, physical, and competitive, while girls are expected to be more emotional, passive, and cooperative. Studies have shown that adults subconsciously behave, react, and interact differently, and in line with gender stereotypes, when interacting with boy versus girl children—even with newborn babies.

In her book *Pink Brain, Blue Brain: How Small Differences Grow into Troublesome Gaps—and What We Can Do About It*, Lise Eliot reviewed hundreds of studies looking at innate differences between genders, including the previously mentioned study in which gender preferences in toys were observed in both monkeys and humans. Eliot claims that these sex-based differences are not typically seen until around age one and explains that there is little evidence for gender differences in the brains of babies. The gender differences we assume, therefore, may be an issue of cultural gender biases, stereotyping (both consciously and subconsciously), and gender conformity.

Regardless of whether nature or nurture is the root cause, there is no denying that differences exist between males and females in our society, and these differences drive both internal and external messages regarding what is expected of us. Messages about gender expectations and stereotypes dictate how a woman *should* be, and as such, render women vulnerable to additional challenges in building self-esteem.

EVALUATING GENDER DIFFERENCES IN YOUR LIFE

When you were growing up, what messages were conveyed to you about what it means to be a girl?

_____

_____

_____

Were there different expectations for males and females in your family of origin? If so, what were they?

_____

_____

_____

What were some positive aspects of being a girl?

_____

_____

_____

Were there any negative aspects of being a girl? If so, what were they?

_____

_____

_____

What differences do you experience now, as an adult?

_____

_____

_____

How have gender differences impacted your self-esteem?

_____

_____

_____

"THE PERFECT WOMAN"

Being a woman in today's society often comes with intense pressure to be perfect. Talk about an unrealistic expectation! Society sends the message that women can and should have it all, do it all, and oh yes, do it all with a smile.

We women have more opportunities today than our great-grandmothers did decades ago. But along with these advancements comes the pressure to do more and seize opportunities, often without guidance as to how we are supposed to manage it all. For example, women today often balance motherhood with a professional identity, as well as involvement in a host of other activities. Seldom is there mention of the fact that women still only have the same 24/7/365 that they did 100 years ago, and so they may have to make sacrifices while juggling all these varied responsibilities, goals, and dreams.

Women, caretakers by nature, end up trying to be everything to everyone. We manage our many roles, often expecting we should be able to do it all on our own. We try to portray the essence of a superwoman, handling everything with ease. And yes, we try to be perfect—the perfect wives, mothers, daughters, sisters, friends, professionals; juggling many balls without letting any of them drop and beating ourselves up if they do!

The trouble here is simple: Perfection is impossible, and perfectionists never feel good enough because they measure everything they do according to what was *not* accomplished rather than what was. They strive to do everything perfectly, and judge themselves as inadequate, broken, or unworthy if they don't meet the mark. Trying to build self-esteem while striving for perfection creates a never-ending cycle of failure, simply because perfection does not exist.

BALANCING ROLES

What are the roles that make up your life? (For example, mother, daughter, sister, aunt, wife, friend, employee, coworker, etc.)

_____

_____

_____

_____

What challenges and stressors have you faced when balancing these various roles?

_____

_____

_____

_____

What emotions does this balancing act bring about? (For example, guilt, frustration, defeat, pride, satisfaction, etc.)

_____

_____

_____

_____

ARE YOU A PERFECTIONIST?

On a scale of 1 to 5, (1 being not at all, and 5 being all the time), rate how often you engage in the following behaviors:

1. **I focus on my failures more than my accomplishments.**

1	2	3	4	5
NOT AT ALL	RARELY	SOMETIMES	OFTEN	ALL THE TIME

2. **I notice my weaknesses more than my strengths.**

1	2	3	4	5
NOT AT ALL	RARELY	SOMETIMES	OFTEN	ALL THE TIME

3. **I set rigid standards for myself.**

1	2	3	4	5
NOT AT ALL	RARELY	SOMETIMES	OFTEN	ALL THE TIME

4. **I have difficulty making decisions.**

1	2	3	4	5
NOT AT ALL	RARELY	SOMETIMES	OFTEN	ALL THE TIME

5. **I tend to seek the approval of others.**

1	2	3	4	5
NOT AT ALL	RARELY	SOMETIMES	(OFFEN)	ALL THE TIME

6. **I rarely feel satisfied with myself or my performance.**

1	2	3	4	5
NOT AT ALL	RARELY	SOMETIMES	(OFTEN)	ALL THE TIME

7. **I struggle with procrastination.**

1	2	3	4	5
NOT AT ALL	RARELY	SOMETIMES	(OFTEN)	ALL THE TIME

8. **I place very strong demands on myself.**

1	2	3	4	5
NOT AT ALL	RARELY	SOMETIMES	(OFTEN)	ALL THE TIME

9. **I am very bothered by mistakes.**

1	2	3	4	5
NOT AT ALL	RARELY	SOMETIMES	(OFTEN)	ALL THE TIME

10. **I become defensive when criticized.**

1	2	3	4	5
NOT AT ALL	RARELY	SOMETIMES	(OFTEN)	ALL THE TIME

Scoring

Add up your score using the following point system:

1 point for every time you marked 1   **Not at all**

2 points for every time you marked 2   **Rarely**

3 points for every time you marked 3   **Sometimes**

4 points for every time you marked 4   **Often**

5 points for every time you marked 5   **All the time**

If you scored anywhere between 35 and 50, it's safe to say you are a perfectionist. It will be important for you to consider the ways in which your perfectionism gets in the way of building self-esteem. If you scored between 20 and 35, you may have a more rational view of yourself; however, perfectionist tendencies still occasionally get in your way, so you can also benefit from watching out for perfectionism. Scoring between 10 and 20 is very rare for somebody with lower self-esteem and could indicate issues with denial or lack of self-awareness.

AN IMPOSSIBLE STANDARD

Women seem to be expected to manage all their roles with perfection, and to do it all while looking perfect, too! One of the biggest and most ludicrous external expectations in our society complicating women's quest for healthy self-esteem is the enormous pressure women face to look and be a certain way. American culture maintains a skewed and unhealthy focus on youth, beauty, and sex appeal, and women receive messages every day that it is important to meet the impossible criteria for what is considered the ideal appearance and body type.

Advertisements and the media make very strong suggestions about what is necessary to be considered "good enough." The message is that you have to be thin, fit, and highly attractive in order to get the attention and approval of others. Positive traits and experiences such as popularity, happiness, confidence, and achievement are linked to beauty and attractiveness, creating even more pressure to meet the ideal beauty standard.

This expectation has many flaws; one of which is that this ideal standard is often impossible to achieve. It has been estimated that most women portrayed in the media are at least 15 percent below the average weight of women, and there is evidence that the ideal body shown in the media has become increasingly thinner over the years. What *isn't* always obvious is the fact that most women in ads are completely unrealistic and sometimes downright fake. There's a saying: *You will never look like the girl in the magazine. The girl in the magazine doesn't even look like the girl in the magazine.* It can be a comfort to know that models themselves are typically airbrushed and altered to perfection; and in some cases, are completely unreal, created as a compilation of different body parts and features from a number of different people! Movie stars have hair and makeup stylists to create a perfect look and personal trainers who spend hours every day focusing on getting their bodies into shape. What we see in ads and on screen, however, is only the final product—women who look effortlessly beautiful, flawless, and perfect in every way. I promise you—they are not.

Regardless, research has shown that we begin internalizing these powerful messages about perfection and what society views as the ideal body type very early in life. For example, studies have looked at the very popular Barbie doll and have demonstrated how completely unrealistic her measurements are, explaining that if Barbie were a real woman, she would be unable to stand up or contain vital human organs due to her awkward proportions and ridiculously small waistline.

We are constantly bombarded with these unrealistic standards and messages urging us to look a certain way. Countless ads for diets, weight-loss pills, cosmetic surgery, makeup, and appearance-altering clothes are ubiquitous in magazines and on TV, suggesting that we, too, must achieve perfection in order to accept ourselves and be accepted. Reality shows depicting makeovers and plastic surgery have become popular, sending the message that you should take control to change anything that may be perceived as a flaw. And as demonstrated in the many ads for wrinkle creams and age-defying products, aging is treated like a disease to be avoided rather than a natural life process that can really be quite beautiful when handled with grace, acceptance, and humor.

EVALUATING YOUR OWN BODY IMAGE

Not surprisingly, women with low self-esteem tend to be particularly critical of themselves, but this is especially true when it comes to body image. Think about your own physical appearance, including things like height, weight, facial features, skin color and quality, hair color, texture, and style, body shape and type, individual body parts, scars, wrinkles, or imperfections, and the way you dress. Make a list of things you feel good about, and then list the things you feel critical of.

Physical qualities I like in myself:

_____
_____
_____
_____

Physical qualities I dislike in myself:

_____
_____
_____
_____

How often do you embrace or feel grateful for your positive qualities?

_____
_____
_____
_____

How much time do you spend feeling self-conscious, criticizing yourself, or ruminating on what you perceive to be flaws?

_____
_____
_____
_____

Which items on the dislike list are you able to control? What measures would it take to make changes, and can you justify these measures as realistic, healthy goals?

_____
_____
_____
_____

APPRECIATING YOUR BODY

As you begin reflecting on the things you like and dislike about your body and appearance, and simultaneously begin paying more attention to society and the media's impact on your self-image, see if you can shift your focus from trying to measure up to impossible standards to appreciating how amazing your body truly is. And rather than focusing on looks, think about all of the things your body does and the ways that different parts of your body help you live and achieve your goals. What are some things you can be appreciative of about your body?

Research has found that body dissatisfaction and self-esteem are closely linked. As one increases, the other decreases, so it's important to begin paying attention to the messages in society that impact your body image and consider how you feel about your own image. Having an appreciation for your body and general contentedness with your appearance are both part of self-esteem; however, having a good and realistic body image doesn't always ensure high self-esteem. It's simply one piece of the puzzle.

LISA'S STORY

Several years ago, I was teaching a workshop on self-esteem and could sense a certain tension in the room when we began discussing body image. The women in the group seemed more reluctant than usual to open up about their own struggles with body image, and I wondered whether it was because there was one member, Lisa, who seemed to stand out among the rest. Lisa met the ideal body type almost to a T. She was thin and very pretty, and I got the sense that others assumed she could not at all relate to issues with body image.

Interestingly, Lisa was the first to begin sharing, opening up about her own struggles with body satisfaction. She shared that accepting her body was a constant battle and that she never quite felt good enough. She revealed that she didn't always have the body type we were observing in the class and explained that for most of her life, she had been very overweight. Several years ago, however, she decided to undergo gastric bypass surgery and liposuction to get rid of the fat.

Lisa described how being thin wasn't all it was cracked up to be. She talked about how, rather than being happy with her new appearance, her focus and hatred of her body simply shifted from being about the excess fat to being about the excess skin that she assured us sagged underneath her clothes.

She talked about how she was treated very differently now than she had been in the past, explaining how people now seem friendlier. They hold the door open for her and stop to chat, whereas they didn't seem to notice her when she was more heavyset. Rather than feel relieved to be experiencing better treatment, she felt sad and angry that society sent the message that her worth was tied to her appearance. "I'm still the same person I always was," she said. "But the way I'm treated differently, better, now makes me struggle even more with self-esteem. If people only knew that what they see isn't the real me, maybe they would think I'm a fraud, stop valuing me, and confirm I have no value."

Lisa worked hard to implement the tools she was learning in order to build self-esteem. Following the workshop, she began individual therapy to further work through her body image and self-esteem issues and started to recognize all the other positive aspects to her identity, apart from her physical appearance. Lisa remained disappointed with the superficiality she witnessed; however, she was able to attribute it to the ignorance of others rather than take it personally.

THE TROUBLE WITH SOCIAL MEDIA

While there have been some attempts to portray more realistic body types in advertising in recent years, such as the Dove Campaign for Real Beauty, which features women of all shapes and sizes, problems with unrealistic ideals are still very present and are amplified by social media, which add to the challenges women face. The unrealistic expectations and portrayals of perfection we see online seep into our subconscious, planting the seed that we, too, need to look and act a certain way. Online, we see pictures, videos, and posts from celebrities, advertisers, and even friends, that again suggest that perfection is the ideal, and we wind up making assumptions that this is the norm. We begin comparing what we see on social media to that in our own lives, often coming up short.

The problem with social media is that we are only seeing a snapshot of a moment in time. People invariably post their best pictures, gush about their happiest moments, and boast about their biggest achievements. We don't see or consider the full picture and instead compare and judge our lives and ourselves against these glimpses of someone else's "perfect" life.

This exposure can create a constant struggle to obtain the unobtainable and lead to an endless search for validation—it's pretty clear how this would pose a challenge to developing healthy self-esteem. Social media lays the groundwork for an obsession with gaining the approval of others. Have you ever tied your worth to how many comments, likes, followers, or views you get on social media? This has the potential to create an environment of inner competition where faulty measures become tied to self-worth.

JOANNE'S STORY

When Joanne, a woman in her late twenties, came to see me, she had a good career, hobbies she enjoyed, her own apartment in a trendy neighborhood, and friends she hung out with on the weekends, yet she was experiencing a great deal of depression and dissatisfaction with her life.

Joanne desperately wanted to be in a relationship but seemed to never have any luck in dating. Initially, I couldn't figure out where she was going wrong. She was likeable, funny, and easy to talk to in sessions. She was attractive and in shape, yet convinced she was overweight and ugly. As I got to know her better, I discovered that deep down she was struggling with self-doubt and low levels of self-esteem, which were likely sabotaging her dating experience.

Joanne had a history of questioning her worth, beating herself up for the smallest things, and always assuming people didn't like her. She spent most of her evenings surfing the Internet, becoming more and more depressed every time she saw news of a Facebook friend's engagement or Instagram pictures of smiling, happy couples. She wondered why everybody else was successful in finding the love and happiness that seemed to elude her and assumed there must be something inherently wrong with her. I suspected that her lack of confidence and anxiety around social interactions came across and was a turnoff to the people she went out with.

I encouraged her to take a break from dating while she focused her energy on working to build self-esteem. We talked a lot about how social media and the interpretations she made without knowing the full picture kept her trapped in all-or-nothing thinking, believing everyone had it better than she did and feeling that she would never fulfill her dreams. It took some time, but Joanne finally began to realize that her constant use of social media was counterproductive to her efforts to overcome her feelings of inadequacy. She made a conscious effort to spend her time more productively, to remember that posts online don't always show the full picture, and to work hard to see the world through a more realistic lens. Eventually, she was able to cut herself some slack and become more patient and kind with herself. As a result, Joanne was able to resume dating with a more open-minded, self-encouraging approach.

EVALUATING SOCIETY'S MESSAGES

Look at ads of women on TV and in magazines and really consider what you see. What do you notice about the models? What messages are conveyed to viewers?

Describe how these ads make you feel:

_____

_____

_____

_____

_____

_____

If you use social media (Facebook, Twitter, Instagram, Tumblr, etc.) go into your accounts and focus on the first several posts you see. What do you notice about the pictures and captions?

_____

_____

_____

_____

How does what you see and read make you feel?

_____

_____

_____

_____

In what ways do you find yourself making comparisons or feeling inadequate?

_____

_____

_____

_____

Does seeing images of fit, beautiful, or happy women motivate or demoralize you?

_____

_____

_____

_____

RESISTING THE PRESSURE TO CONFORM

External expectations, impossible standards, portrayals of perfection, and social pressures—they all come together to create an environment that makes it very challenging for women to feel adequate and worthy as we are. But when we can't accept our own shortcomings, we are failing to acknowledge our very humanity. The impossible quest to measure up to unrealistic archetypes sets women up to feel like failures; it's up to us as individuals to feel good about who we are despite those outside influences. If those influences make you start to believe there is something fundamentally wrong with you, it can take an incredible toll on self-esteem.

In order to begin building self-esteem, it's important to resist the pressure to conform—to unrealistic standards, to the portrayal of the perfect woman, to the gender stereotypes and pressures in our culture—to all of it! We need to be realistic about who we are and what we can achieve. The reality is, we simply are not perfect, and we cannot always have and do it all. But we can love and accept ourselves the way we are, limitations and flaws included.

There will probably always be idealized but unrealistic messages and pressures in society, but you can make the conscious choice to stop letting them control how you think and feel. This shift starts with becoming more aware of how you are impacted by these expectations, separating yourself from negative messaging that hinders your self-image, and being more realistic about what to expect of yourself with regard to what you can and cannot change.

You can begin to shift toward a stance of nonconformity by focusing on your own goals and what is important to you, rather than on what you think everyone else expects you to be. As you map out your goals, ensure that they are realistic, achievable, and yours. Be gentle with your assessment of yourself and others. Think about and practice the following action steps:

1. Resist the pressure to conform
2. Resist the urge to compare
3. Be careful not to unfairly judge
4. Stop fearing judgment from others
5. Recognize that you are not perfect

Other Societal Barriers

In addition to biological and socialized gender gaps, hormonal inconveniences, and the onslaught of skewed messaging in society, women continue to face things like ageism, sexism, and institutional barriers that challenge our sense of identities.

While men, too, face potentially demoralizing messages in society and advertising, there seems to be a greater burden on women, particularly when it comes to the pressure to be attractive and thin and to avoid aging. As men age, they are often depicted as distinguished and wise, while aging women are more often depicted as old, washed-out, and incapable. For women, aging and the ticking of the biological clock is something we have been taught to fear. All of this pressure creates a major dilemma for women, who have to grapple with the discrepancies between reality and the impossible standard.

Let's now consider our patriarchal society, in which women sometimes find themselves ignored, overlooked, or discriminated against, especially in the workforce. Stigmas from the past linger, implying that women are weak, overly emotional, and mentally inferior. Often, women do not receive the same level of respect men do, and they are sometimes unfairly mocked for biologically driven factors, like talking too much, menstrual mood swings, and being "overly" sensitive.

In the workplace, women continue to earn less, making approximately two-thirds what men do for similar work. Men tend to have more powerful, higher-status positions. Outspoken men are labeled as assertive, while women who speak up are labeled as bitchy. Women also face problems with sexism, sexual harassment, and sexual assault more often than men, and are sometimes the butt of derogatory and demeaning jokes. These things can create shame, self-consciousness, and distress, and lead women to ultimately question their value.

As I write this, we are in the wake of the #MeToo campaign that's spread across the world, detailing countless allegations of sexual harassment and misconduct toward women. This movement highlights the magnitude of the problem with sexual harassment and shows how unfair and demeaning treatment toward women can potentially break their spirits. Barriers like gender discrimination and unfair biases toward women hamper success and can make it difficult for women to maintain healthy self-esteem.

To better illustrate how women can stay trapped in a place of low self-esteem when facing sexist treatment, read the following scenario:

SUZANNE AND CAROLINE

Suzanne and Caroline both work for the same boss, Larry. Larry is egotistical, abrasive, and very chauvinistic. He frequently comments on their appearance, saying things like, "Nice dress" or "You look lovely today." While his comments are typically complimentary, both women feel uncomfortable. They feel as if they are under a microscope and feel pressure to keep up a perfect appearance at work.

Larry never comments on the appearance of male colleagues. Further, he frequently singles out the female employees to do things like fetch his coffee, order lunch for client meetings, and make travel arrangements, while the male counterparts are never tasked with these requests. At company happy hours, Larry is known to drink one too many and begin cracking jokes that are demeaning to women. At times, he becomes overly flirtatious with Suzanne and Caroline, calling them "sweetie" and "hon."

Suzanne, a woman with low self-esteem, constantly feels uncomfortable around her boss but assumes that's just the way it is. While taking lunch orders or making travel arrangements, she tells herself she probably just isn't as good as some of her peers who handle more important responsibilities. She thinks, "I'm just not smart enough. If I were, my boss would treat me with more respect and give me more challenging work."

Caroline, on the other hand, has a healthy level of self-esteem. "My boss is an arrogant, sexist jerk. I don't deserve to put up with his BS," she tells herself as she debates whether to confront her boss, talk to HR, or look for another job where her talents will be appreciated.

Do you relate more to Caroline or Suzanne? Why?

_____

_____

_____

_____

How do you think you would react in the same situation?

_____

_____

_____

_____

As shown in this scenario, sexism and gender discrimination interact with the ability to maintain self-esteem. When the foundation of self-esteem is strong, it is easier to deal with things like biases, misogyny, and unfair treatment. However, when self-esteem is already low, these challenges aid in further depleting self-esteem, serving as barriers to making positive changes.

Developing a better understanding of the obstacles you face as a woman in our society opens you up to a greater level of awareness that will serve you well as we delve into part 2 and learn tools to help build self-esteem. By acknowledging the conscious and subconscious challenges you face, you become better prepared to ultimately push past these obstacles and make your way toward improved self-esteem.

IN YOUR EXPERIENCE

It's important to recognize that even the subtlest encounter can influence your self-image. As you look at the following list, check off anything you have experienced and consider how these incidents play a role in your ability to build and maintain self-esteem.

I have:

- ☐ Been subjected to jokes of a sexual or demeaning nature
- ☐ Experienced unwanted touching
- ☐ Experienced unwanted sexual advances
- ☐ Been pressured into sexual activity
- ☐ Been solicited for sexual favors
- ☐ Faced humiliation related to gender or sexuality
- ☐ Been criticized for appearance
- ☐ Been shamed for sexual activity
- ☐ Been mocked for declining to engage in sexual activity
- ☐ Received unwanted inappropriate pictures
- ☐ Witnessed lewd or offensive gestures
- ☐ Been subjected to nudity or witnessed masturbation in public
- ☐ Been sexually assaulted or raped

How have these experiences impacted your self-esteem or your view of yourself?

_____

_____

_____

_____

We have explored how our experiences play a tremendous role in shaping who we are and how we feel about ourselves. It can be difficult to look in the face of past experiences when they carry painful weight. But just know that by facing those issues head-on, perhaps reflecting on them or writing about them, you have taken a massive first step in the right direction—you have acknowledged burdens that have, up to this point, likely stood in your way of progress. We will now turn our attention to the five steps we can take to move toward healthy self-esteem. Give yourself a hug. You are awesome. Now, together, let's move on to the steps!

·········

PART TWO

5 STEPS TO HEALTHY SELF-ESTEEM

N THE PREVIOUS SECTION, we looked at what self-esteem is and gained a better understanding of some of the challenges you may face as you begin working to improve your level of self-esteem. This section details five steps that will walk you through the journey of gaining inner strength and creating the happier, more confident life you deserve. Each step contains different ways in which you can explore your self-image and your relationships, most especially the relationship you have with yourself, in order to pinpoint factors that may play a role in the development of your self-esteem.

You will gain valuable insight, discover new tools, and receive guidance for making positive, lasting changes. Prompts and exercises will help you discover which aspects of your life have contributed to low self-esteem, and specific action items will help you begin to immediately implement what you've learned—this will help motivate you as you create your personal foundation of healthy self-esteem.

Every step is important to the journey, so please take your time with each one, and remember there are no prescribed time frames for any of the steps, exercises, or action items. Your journey will be unique, requiring its own, individual amount of time. Healthy self-esteem involves a whole lot of being kind to yourself, so have patience and give yourself the space you need to effectively process and work through each step before moving on to the next. At the same time, strive to find the courage and willpower to step outside your comfort zone—even in small ways—and try out new behaviors and ways of thinking.

You will get from these steps whatever you put into them, so again, take your time to read through each chapter, and be as thoughtful as possible as you answer the questions and complete the exercises. Be sure to complete the "Look Back to Move Forward" section at the end of each chapter before beginning a new step.

Know Yourself

KNOWING YOURSELF IS THE FIRST STEP to building your self-esteem. When you have a solid grasp of who you are today, where you have come from, and what experiences have impacted your self-image, you can move forward toward improved self-esteem. Self-awareness allows you to identify where you lack self-esteem, understand exactly how low self-esteem negatively impacts your life, and make changes to improve self-esteem. This step involves getting in touch with who you really are, and the process can be transformative. From there, you can begin really taking ownership of your life and readily understand and change any negative aspects that may have contributed to low self-esteem.

As we begin, stop for a moment and write a few sentences describing who you are:

_____

_____

_____

_____

_____

What emotions did you experience as you were trying to describe and summarize who you are? Did you find it difficult?

_____

_____

_____

_____

Women with healthy self-esteem usually know themselves well. They acknowledge both their strengths and weaknesses, recognize the various factors that have played a role in their development, and generally feel in control of their lives. They take responsibility for personal courses of action, despite how others may act, and are able to separate external influences from their core sense of self. This encompasses characteristics like independent-mindedness, security, and not being overly sensitive.

Conversely, women with low self-esteem have become disconnected from their own self. They see themselves through a faulty lens, and sometimes view themselves as simply an extension of other people. They often neglect to cultivate their own identity and tend to routinely sacrifice their own identities to care for others. By nature, women are nurturing caretakers and good at tending to the needs of others; however, when a woman endures years of low self-esteem, she becomes susceptible to taking care of everyone but herself.

Women with low self-esteem may constantly try to please others while losing themselves in the process. Take, for example, a woman who hates sports but pretends to love football so the new guy she's dating thinks she's cool and fun. She ends up doing things like this to please others and be accepted, to the point that she forgets who she really is and what she truly likes and dislikes. When you become so far removed from your own thoughts, ideas, and opinions, it becomes difficult to remember or recognize who you are. Identifying even very basic likes and dislikes can become a challenge.

Part of knowing yourself involves refamiliarizing yourself with who you truly are today. The following exercise allows you to spend some time thinking about your own identity, including what you like and what your hopes and dreams are.

Watch out for any thoughts that might pop up regarding the expectations, demands, or desires of others; instead, answer the following questions based solely on your own gut and intuition. It may take some time to come up with answers, but that's okay. Take your time and answer any questions you can, and feel free to skip over ones that seem too difficult to complete at this stage.

A Few of My Favorite Things

My favorite color is: _____

My favorite food is: _____

My favorite place is: _____

My favorite activity is: _____

My favorite hobby or interest is: _____

My favorite show, movie, or book is: _____

My favorite music is: _____

When I have alone time, I like to: _____

If I could choose anywhere to go, it would be to: _____

As a young girl, I wanted to be: _____

My dream job now would be: _____

If I could have dinner with anyone, I would choose: _____

One of my favorite memories is: _____

One of my greatest accomplishments is: _____

One of my greatest challenges has been: _____

A defining moment in my life was: _____

Now reflect on the process of answering the questions. Did it take you a short or long time to think of responses? If you found it difficult, what did you experience? Did you feel a sense of disconnect in remembering who you are? What thoughts came up as you were answering?

_____

_____

_____

_____

OLIVIA'S STORY

Olivia, a woman in her early 50s, began therapy to deal with the depression she felt after being laid off from her job as an administrative assistant, a position she'd held for nearly 20 years. She didn't know where to begin in terms of searching for a new job or finding a different path for her future.

As I got to know her, I discovered Olivia's days were mostly spent alone at home. It was obvious she felt lonely and unfulfilled, and she blamed depression for preventing her from making any changes. We talked about what things had been like when she was working: Olivia liked the security of a paycheck and the routine that her job provided, but couldn't pinpoint any specific aspects of her work she particularly enjoyed.

Olivia had a difficult time answering many of my questions regarding what her goals were, what type of work she might enjoy, and what her hobbies and interests were. It became apparent that Olivia was completely disconnected from who she was, due to years of suffering with low self-esteem.

For decades, Olivia had gone about her day-to-day routine, getting up, going to work, coming home, watching TV, and going to bed. She accomplished her work and was friendly with her coworkers but didn't feel challenged or particularly bonded with anyone. I began noticing that Olivia struggled with making the simplest of decisions on her own; a problem that would certainly make it difficult for her to change her situation.

We started digging deeper into her history and discovered that a chaotic childhood with years of feeling unimportant to her parents had set her up to constantly feel inadequate and unable to push herself toward greater goals. She'd learned to fade into the shadows and stay out of the way. As an adult, Olivia repeated these behaviors and became more and more out of touch with who she was, what she liked, and what she wanted.

In order to get relief from her depression and make choices that would move her forward, she needed to go back to the basics and discover who she was, what she liked, and what she wanted for her future. In the process, she began to let go of years of personal blame and open herself up to rediscovering who she was. As she gradually began getting in touch with her own likes, dislikes, interests, and dreams, she began to build self-esteem and feel ready to make changes to improve her quality of life.

Do you identify with Olivia? In what ways?

_____

_____

_____

_____

Do you ever have difficulty making decisions or expressing your likes and dislikes?

_____

_____

_____

_____

Are there any aspects of your life that have become so habitual and routine that you feel you've lost your sense of purpose or excitement?

_____

_____

_____

_____

Influences That Shape Self-Esteem

Our self-esteem begins to develop early in life and is based in part on the messages we receive and interpret from the significant people in our lives. We assign meaning to the various things we hear and observe. These memories are stored and coded in our brains in ways that influence our individual view of self-image. The foundation of self-esteem forms early in childhood, but it can be changed and shaped by everything we continue to experience throughout our lives.

Part of knowing yourself involves exploring the various influences that contribute to your perception of self-worth and impact your internal core view of who you are. In this section, we will start by looking into your past experiences to determine what messages you received growing up. Making the connection to past experiences that contributed to establishing the roots of your self-esteem can help you work through challenges that stand in your way in the present. Often, people don't realize that their current struggles stem from past circumstances. If you discover this to be true for you, just know that it is never too late to learn tools and make changes that can greatly enhance your level of self-esteem and transform the course of your future.

MY TIMELINE

BIRTH

In the space provided or on a large piece of paper, create a timeline of your life, from birth to present. Plot some of the significant life experiences that may have impacted your self-esteem.

What thoughts and ideas does this picture generate?

_____

_____

_____

_____

As young children, we don't yet have the capacity to recognize that our worth is not determined by what others say or do, yet we are impressionable and learn lessons from everything we experience and witness. We internalize every message we encounter as we form our sense of personal identity. Whether intentional or inadvertent, messages that are interpreted as negative or hurtful can harm self-esteem. Research demonstrates that our brains are naturally wired with a negativity bias; this means we give more weight to the negative

PRESENT

information and experiences in our lives than we do to the positives. Therefore, even just a handful of negative experiences can contribute to low self-esteem.

Think back on your own past memories and jot down the first few that come to mind:

_____

_____

_____

_____

What stands out more—positive, happy memories, or ones that involve negative feelings or moments?

_____

_____

_____

_____

We interpret and internalize messages about every experience throughout our lives. These messages can come in the form of verbal communications, nonverbal cues, and our own translations of the actions or inactions of others. Messages may be loud and clear, or they may be subtle. They are also subject to misinterpretation. Regardless of how messages are intended, our interpretations may ultimately impact our self-esteem. Sometimes messages can even be mixed; this can create issues of identity confusion that get in the way of our ability to form healthy self-esteem.

For example, your parent may tell you, "I love you," but never show up for the important events in your life. You could take this to mean they don't care about you and deem youself unlovable. Or you might feel slighted if a friend declines your attempts to play together and misinterpret the slight to mean that you are not likable. As children, we are vulnerable to taking everything personally. We cannot always see rational explanations or alternatives, such as, "My single mother didn't show up because she is busy working two jobs to make ends meet" and "The friend who didn't want to play is busy or not feeling well today."

When we infer negative and self-disparaging meaning from our experiences, we sabotage our own sense of worth. Low self-esteem is often the result of years of internalizing negative messages and developing a habit of questioning our own value. As a result, we stay trapped in a never-ending cycle of doubting ourselves, taking everything personally, and interpreting various scenarios in a way that perpetuates our perceived lack of self-worth.

Do you remember any personal experiences that may have hurt your sense of worth?

_____

_____

_____

_____

ERICA'S STORY

Erica complained about difficulties she was having with her interpersonal relationships. She had many close friends, yet she always seemed to be clashing with somebody. As she talked about her friendships and various conflicts, I started to see that her expectations of others were quite high, and her friends' ability to live up to these expectations seemed tied to her own self-worth.

Erica became jealous anytime she discovered two of her friends got together without her. Once, she came to a session raging that she'd realized via social media that her best friend, Sara, had lunch with their other friend, Emily. "How could they not invite me?" she fumed.

When I saw her the following week, I learned the lunch had not been planned in advance. Sara and Emily had run into each other in a store and decided to grab a quick bite before continuing on with their individual errands. Unfortunately, before finding out this information, Erica had already sent them both an angry and sarcastic text message, saying, "Thanks a lot for the invite to lunch."

Erica was prone to jumping to conclusions anytime she felt left out or disconnected from her group of friends. If she hadn't heard from friends for a few days or messaged them and did not immediately hear back, she assumed they were hanging out without her and intentionally excluding her from the fun. I worried that if Erica's paranoia and tendency to lash out at her friends continued, she was going to create a self-fulfilling prophecy in which her friends no longer wanted to deal with her high-maintenance friendship.

I encouraged Erica to think back to other times in her life when she experienced similar feelings of being left out. She identified times during high school when she felt annoyed that her dad rarely made it to her volleyball games. Growing up, she and her brother, Brad, were both athletic, but Brad's football games frequently overlapped with her volleyball games. Their dad, an avid football fan, never missed a football game, leaving Erica needing to rely on others for rides to games and feeling disappointed that he wasn't there to cheer her on.

Rationally, Erica knew her dad couldn't be in two places at once, but his lack of interest in attending her games, coupled with lingering sadness from her childhood years regarding her dad frequently being away on business trips, left Erica feeling unimportant in his eyes.

As she got back in touch with these painful and vulnerable feelings from her past, she realized that her anger toward her friends reflected the disappointment she felt regarding feeling ignored by her dad. At the root of her jealous tendencies in her friendships was a desperate attempt to avoid feeling neglected. Her need to feel valued was an attempt to disprove the messages she'd internalized growing up—those that told her she was unimportant and not worthy.

As Erica processed these feelings, she worked through her hurt from the past and was able to separate it from her present-day interactions, allowing her to feel more confident in herself and secure in her relationships.

Can you relate to any aspects of Erica's story?

_____

_____

_____

Do you ever feel left out or paranoid about whether people in your life like you?

_____

_____

_____

_____

Do you ever react in extreme or impulsive ways due to beliefs that might be irrational or unwarranted?

_____

_____

_____

_____

Family Factors

From the day we're born, the people around us convey messages that we internalize to form our core belief system about ourselves and the world around us. Therefore, it's no surprise that women with unhealthy role models and less nurturing caretakers would be more prone to developing low self-esteem. Women who grow up in environments involving dysfunction, addiction, or abuse tend to be more vulnerable to internalizing feelings of worthlessness. Women with parents who are critical toward themselves or others are likely to be highly self-critical, and women whose families conveyed the message that it was not okay to express feelings can develop identity confusion and feelings of wrongdoing that lead to problems with low self-esteem.

Did you experience any of the following things in your family of origin?

☐ Abuse (physical, emotional, sexual) ☐ Lack of emotional expression
☐ Addiction   ☐ Fear of expressing emotion
☐ Frequent angry outbursts   ☐ Criticism
☐ Dysfunction   ☐ Hostile sarcasm
☐ Poor communication   ☐ Unclear expectations

Unfortunately, dysfunction and maladaptive patterns can be passed down for generations. If any of these issues are part of your history, don't be discouraged. By developing an awareness of the problem, you have already taken the first step in breaking that cycle and making lasting improvements.

If you are somebody who grew up with a healthy childhood and marked none of the boxes in the Family Factors exercise, you may find yourself wondering where your low self-esteem could possibly have come from. Know that it's not just women with troubled backgrounds who struggle with low self-esteem. Even healthy, nurturing families can inadvertently contribute to problems with low self-esteem. Unintentional messages and actions by even the most loving of parents can sometimes send messages that create feelings of self-doubt and inadequacy. For example, a busy parent may unintentionally ignore a child while tending to other responsibilities to support the family. In turn, the child may internalize this lack of attention to mean they are unimportant or not cared about. When a child routinely experiences these types of disappointments, it can hinder development of healthy self-esteem.

Write about any times you remember feeling unimportant in your family.

_____

_____

_____

_____

_____

_____

In some cases, family members and others are simply doing the best they can, based on their own current stressors and their own upbringing, life experiences, and level of self-esteem. However, when we're young, or have already formed low self-esteem, we are incapable of seeing things objectively. In this case, actions by others that we interpret as hurtful can create deep-seated internal conflicts that interfere with identity and self-worth.

THE IMPACT OF FAMILY

Think about your history, the experiences you've encountered, and the messages you received in childhood as you complete the following sentences:

Growing up, I felt: _____

My parents or caretakers were: _____

My relationships with my siblings were: _____

Being a girl in my family was: _____

The best aspects of my childhood were: _____

The worst parts of my childhood were: _____

Look over your responses. Do any of them appear to be factors that could have played a role in hindering healthy self-esteem? Looking at family history can sometimes offer insight on the early origins of problems with low self-esteem and related present-day struggles. You may or may not notice factors in your family history that could have contributed to low self-esteem. It is sometimes difficult or even impossible to pinpoint exactly where low self-esteem stems from. Regardless, it is absolutely still possible to build self-esteem up, even when the cause is unknown.

Outside Influences

Most research on this subject focuses on how families of origin create legacies of self-criticism and low self-esteem in women, but it's not just our immediate families that influence the way we perceive ourselves. Our self-esteem in both childhood and adulthood is also impacted by things we experience in external settings. These experiences can occur within our own relationships as well as in what we witness in the world around us. Interactions with teachers, coaches, peers, friends, extended family, and even strangers all have the ability to impact our self-esteem.

Not surprisingly, things like bullying, abuse, and dealings with narcissistic people create vulnerabilities with regard to self-esteem. Additionally, overt or even implied criticism or ridicule by anyone we encounter can make us question our value. As we explored in the previous chapter, what we view outside our immediate network, in society, can also impact how we feel about ourselves as we equate various expectations with value and worth.

It would be easy to develop and maintain self-esteem if we were shielded from any external influences, but the reality is, *everything* we experience has the ability to impact our self-esteem, whether negatively or positively. As we move through childhood, adolescence, and adulthood, we are constantly receiving messages about what is considered acceptable and desirable, and so we make comparisons and question whether our own identity fits the bill.

Did you experience any of these things in childhood? Check the boxes if applicable:

☐ Abuse (physical, emotional, sexual)   ☐ Bullying
☐ Criticism   ☐ Dealing with a narcissist
☐ Ridicule   ☐ Dealing with somebody irrational

To complicate matters, the same things that challenge our self-esteem can also *become* challenges in and of themselves when self-esteem is not in a healthy place. Things like dating, working, taking on responsibilities, and inter-acting with different people open us up to new experiences that can shape our self-esteem. If self-esteem is already low, navigating these experiences can be difficult. Without a foundation of healthy self-esteem, even simple interactions can perpetuate doubt about who we are as we continue to interpret and assign negative meaning to our every interaction and internalize this negativity.

STACEY'S STORY

Stacey was a young woman struggling with anxiety and bouts of depression that created frequent suicidal thoughts. We had a hard time pinpointing where her anxiety and depression stemmed from—she had a loving and supportive family, a wide network of friends, and a job she enjoyed. Despite a life that looked great on paper, Stacey struggled with assertiveness, making decisions, and perfectionism, constantly second-guessing herself and beating herself up for even the most minor mistakes.

With some clients, it's easy to see where their self-critical voice comes from—it's often a reflection of the messages they heard growing up or a result of some traumatic experience. Stacey, however, could recall no such turmoil. Her family was wonderful, her parents supportive, and her siblings caring and successful. Her childhood had been happy. She was at a loss for where she'd gone wrong. There was, however, one memory that stood out for her as being particularly bad.

Back in high school, Stacey, a very talented artist, was working on a painting in her art class when her art teacher suggested she change the colors on her canvas. Stacey declined to make the change, saying she was happy with her work and wanted to keep the colors closer to the original she was replicating. The teacher proceeded to rip the canvas off the easel and throw it in the sink under running water. Shocked, Stacey ran out of the classroom and found it difficult to return to class next week. The teacher never said anything about the incident.

The event had been scarring. While it may not have been the root of Stacey's struggles with self-esteem, it was a traumatic encounter that stayed with her for years, contributing to her self-doubt and preventing her from trusting her own gut instincts.

Objectively, it was easy for me to surmise that the teacher was facing some personal issue that caused her to inappropriately lash out and project onto Stacey. Yet Stacey had a hard time stepping back from the raw emotions to see herself as merely a victim of a teacher's unprofessional actions. Instead, she felt targeted as flawed and wrong, and couldn't escape the feelings of shame and guilt that still lingered.

Through therapy, Stacey began to see that there was more to her life than the isolated negative incident her mind ruminated on. She worked to see the bigger picture surrounding negative experiences and eventually came to recognize that she could trust and respect her own perspective.

Do you relate to anything in Stacey's story?

_____

_____

_____

_____

Do you have any strong memories that were particularly humiliating or shameful?

_____

_____

_____

_____

If you were able to identify any negative memories, do you find it difficult to see the experience(s) from other perspectives besides that of your own hurt and embarrassment?

_____

_____

_____

_____

Early Messages That Shape Self-Esteem

As you develop a greater awareness of who you are and how your past shaped your current level of self-esteem, it will be useful to explore some of the messages you may have internalized growing up. As you read through the following list of messages, check the boxes by any items that stand out as feeling true for you.

These do not have to be messages you heard aloud; rather, they might be things you interpreted based on what you observed, encountered, or experienced. Don't become overly involved in logic or reasoning, just check what resonates for you from an emotional standpoint. Also keep in mind that you may have received mixed messages or different messages from different people at different times in your life, so it's perfectly fine to check two messages that seem like opposites.

Growing up, I felt:

☐ Liked	☐ Disliked
☐ Unconditionally loved	☐ Unloved or loved conditionally
☐ Wanted	☐ Unwanted
☐ Appreciated	☐ Unappreciated or underappreciated
☐ Trusted	☐ Doubted, suspected, or disbelieved
☐ Valued	☐ Rejected
☐ Cared for physically	☐ Neglected physically
☐ Cared for emotionally	☐ Neglected emotionally
☐ Protected	☐ Ignored or abandoned
☐ Smart	☐ Stupid
☐ Good	☐ Bad
☐ Giving	☐ Selfish
☐ Like a priority	☐ Like a burden or a nuisance
☐ Free to be independent	☐ Like an object to make others happy
☐ Able to make mistakes	☐ A need to be perfect
☐ Able to show my feelings	☐ A need to hide my feelings
☐ Attractive	☐ Unattractive
☐ Happy	☐ Sad
☐ Acceptable	☐ Flawed and inadequate
☐ Successful	☐ Like a failure
☐ Important	☐ Unimportant
☐ Like a source of pride	☐ Like a disappointment or embarrassment
☐ Capable	☐ Incompetent
☐ Labeled as delightful	☐ Labeled as a troublemaker

As you look over your checkmarks, note whether there is an imbalance in checks across the two columns. People with healthy self-esteem will most likely have more checks in the left-hand column, while people with low self-esteem will either have more checks in the right-hand column or a mix across columns that contribute to a sense of identity confusion, causing difficulties with self-esteem.

Self-Talk and Self-Criticism

The messages that we receive and internalize in childhood become a part of our view of ourselves and contribute to the tone of our inner voice or what is frequently referred to as *self-talk*. Our self-talk is comprised of everything we think throughout our day, both consciously and subconsciously. All day we think things to ourselves—we give ourselves feedback, reflect upon various encounters, and contemplate details of past, present, and future endeavors.

Stop for a moment and think about what thoughts are going through your mind right now as you read this.

I am thinking:

_____

_____

_____

_____

It may be difficult to identify thoughts or put them on paper because we aren't used to paying close attention to our every thought or forming thoughts into complete words and sentences. But even when specific thoughts are not at the forefront of our minds, we are still thinking. You may be focused on the words you are reading, yet a part of your mind is still thinking and processing information—thinking about whether you agree with what you read, whether it makes sense, or how you may be able to relate to what you are learning. You may be thinking, *"This feels ridiculous"* or *"I don't think I'm thinking anything."* But those thoughts are exactly what I'm talking about. It's your inner dialogue and the flurry of thoughts on your mind that make up self-talk.

Some people describe self-talk as "a little voice" in their mind, and if you're not typically introspective, you might admit that recognizing it makes you feel a little crazy; but in reality, self-talk is a very normal thing. It's something we all engage in, and it's not the same thing as being delusional or having schizophrenia. It's simply a part of being human and having an evolved brain—and for the record, it can be a wonderful gift to have. Your conscience, your values, your intuition—they are all tied to self-talk. In fact, developing your awareness of self-talk is an important step to getting to know yourself and becoming more conscientious about how you think. The best part is, when you program your self-talk in positive ways, it can be your greatest cheerleader and a driver for success.

Write about times you've been aware of a little voice in your mind. What did that voice say?

_____

_____

_____

_____

Self-Talk and Early Messages

Self-talk is often shaped by the messages we hear or infer growing up, sometimes even directly reflecting the voices we heard as children. If you routinely received or sensed criticisms from others, you are more prone to having developed a strong, critical inner voice that echoes the judgment you encountered—or continue to encounter—from other people. As you begin listening to your own inner voice, pay attention to times that your self-talk seems to reflect or mimic the messages you received or believed about yourself earlier in life.

A Voice from the Past

Reflect on the checklist of Early Messages That Shape Self-Esteem (page 79), and write about times you find your self-talk echoing messages from your past or mirroring other people in your life:

_____

_____

_____

_____

Self-Esteem and Negative Self-Talk

Women with low self-esteem typically have patterns of thinking that are habitually negative, especially regarding thoughts that are personal and self-focused. If it gets out of hand, self-talk can be like an internal critic that judges our every move. The internal critic for women with low self-esteem tends to be overly judgmental and extremely self-belittling. If you have low self-esteem, you likely beat yourself up, second-guess your decisions, and harshly criticize your every move through a constant stream of negative self-talk.

Remember the example of Suzanne and Caroline (page 57)? Each woman faced the same situation with their sexually harassing boss, Larry; however, the differences in their self-esteem and their self-talk contributed to the differences in how they felt and responded.

The idea behind self-talk is that it's not actual events that control how we feel, it's how we *think* about an event or situation that determines our moods, emotions, and ultimate courses of action. Suzanne became consumed with thoughts of not being good or smart enough. She felt powerless and stayed stuck in a position where she was undervalued and even sexually harassed. Caroline, on the other hand, faced the situation with thoughts about how she didn't deserve that type of treatment. She decided to take action and make changes to better her future. The following scenario provides another example of how impactful self-talk can be.

REBECCA AND SHANNON

Rebecca and Shannon have plans to meet for lunch. They greet each other at the hostess stand and wait to be seated.

Rebecca thinks, "I really like Shannon's dress." "Cute dress!" she says.

"Thanks. I've had it forever." Shannon says, thinking, "I wonder if she's just saying that to be nice. She probably notices I've gained some weight since we last saw each other."

The friends are seated at a table and start catching up on what's been going on in each of their lives when the waiter comes to ask for their drink orders.

"I'm really thirsty after my run this morning," *Rebecca thinks. She orders water.*

"Shoot," *thinks Shannon.* "I really wanted a soda. But she's just having water. She's so healthy. If I order a soda she may judge me for all the sugar. Especially if she did notice I gained a few pounds. I really want a soda though. But then I'll owe more money. Paying the bill might be awkward. I don't want her to have to pay extra." *"I'll have a water, too," she tells the waiter.*

"What are you thinking of getting?" Rebecca asks as she looks at the menu.

"I don't know yet. What about you?" Shannon responds. "I hope she decides first so I can decide. I was thinking about the burger, but I don't want to get that if she's just getting a salad or something."

"I'm in the mood for pasta," *Rebecca thinks, then states, "I'm thinking of the pasta."*

"Okay, if she gets pasta I can probably get a burger. They are about the same price point and I won't seem as much like a glutton if she's getting an entrée. Though maybe I should just get the pasta, too, even though I had pasta for dinner last night. No, wait, then she might think I'm copying her. Okay, back to the burger. Shoot, the waiter's coming back," *Shannon thinks.*

She orders the burger and feels a slight sense of relief after having that decision out of the way. But her anxiety comes back as the two friends begin chatting. Throughout the meal, Shannon is filled with similar anxious self-talk, internally questioning whether she is saying the right things and fearing that she might appear foolish for something she says or does.

Rebecca's self-talk, on the other hand, is relatively calm. She thinks how nice it is to catch up, how much she likes the painting on the wall, and whether she might be able to find a similar pasta recipe online.

When the meal is over and the bill comes, Rebecca barely notices, continuing with the story she'd been telling.

"I wonder if I should put my credit card in now," *thinks Shannon.* "If I reach for my wallet, she might think I'm rushing to leave. I don't want her to think I'm bored or uninterested. I'll just wait. But then what if she notices the bill and thinks I'm expecting her to pay for me since I haven't put money in yet? Maybe I'll wait until there's a break in the conversation. I wonder if she's planning to use a credit card, too. Oh no, maybe I should have brought cash."

As Rebecca finishes her story, she reaches into her purse and pulls out her credit card. Shannon follows her lead and does the same. The two split the check, get ready to leave, and say their goodbyes.

As Shannon drives home, she rehashes the lunch date in her mind, considering whether there was anything she had said or done wrong. "I probably sounded so stupid when I told her that story about my job. Why did I even talk about that? I wonder if Rebecca really even likes me. We've been friends since high school, but maybe she just hangs out with me because she feels sorry for me or it's just out of habit. She probably asked other people to lunch first and nobody else could go. I wonder if we'd even be friends if we met today. Man, I'm really craving a soda. I should have just gotten a soda. Anyone else would have just ordered what they really wanted without thinking twice about it. I don't know why I can't just handle simple things. I'm so crazy and ridiculous. Why is everything so hard for me?"

Rebecca leaves thinking, "That pasta was good and it was great to see Shannon. I really need to grab lunch with friends more often!" *Her thoughts then turn to what she has on her agenda for the rest of the afternoon.*

Who do you identify with more, Rebecca or Shannon?

_____

_____

What types of self-talk do you notice in your everyday encounters? Can you provide some examples?

_____

_____

_____

_____

The example of Shannon and Rebecca shows two young women who are in very different places with their levels of self-esteem. Low self-esteem for Shannon dictates her pattern of self-talk and keeps her trapped in a place of anxiety, where she constantly doubts herself and second-guesses her every move. Much of her time and energy is spent analyzing everything she says and does, dwelling on mistakes she may have made. Rebecca, on the other hand, has a healthy level of self-esteem. She does not engage in self-deprecating thinking. Rather, her mental energy is spent enjoying the moment. She is able to make decisions independently and feel confident about her interactions.

Can you identify any other benefits to having self-talk more consistent with Rebecca's?

_____

_____

_____

_____

In the next section, we will look at some distinct ways in which negative self-talk may show up for you. But before we move on, I want to ask you to take some time to pay attention to your own patterns of thinking during a recent encounter you may have had with a friend, family member, or coworker. Write a few sentences about your own frame of mind and the nature of your internal dialogue during that social encounter. Were you filled with anxiety and self-doubt? Or did you enjoy the moment?

Experience: (What, where, with whom?)

_____

_____

_____

_____

What I noticed about my self-talk:

_____

_____

_____

_____

Distorted and Irrational Thinking

With low self-esteem, it's easy to fall into a habit of engaging in negative self-talk that includes distorted and irrational thinking. Over time, this habit expands, and self-talk becomes full of negative messages that sabotage your chances of feeling confident or worthy. You may become unable to navigate situations without anxiety and self-doubt, and may be consumed by thoughts that further destroy self-esteem. This can cause you to become trapped in a downward spiral of negative thinking.

When something goes wrong, low self-esteem can prevent you from seeing the situation objectively. You may assume everything is your fault and become incapable of seeing the bigger picture, a perspective based solely on feelings that you are bad, wrong, or unworthy. Rather than realizing the boss is going through a difficult divorce, the cashier was just diagnosed with cancer, or your friend is having a bad day, you may assume any conflict you encounter has to do with something wrong with *you*.

Distorted thinking can show up in a number of different ways that can be divided into the following categories. These descriptions demonstrate some of the most common patterns of dysfunctional thinking, with specific examples of negative self-talk messages. As you read through each description, contemplate your own style of thinking. If you identify with any of the categories, give examples of times when you tend to engage in this type of thinking.

THE MANY SHAPES OF DISTORTED THINKING

Black or White Thinking

Black or white thinking occurs when you see things in extreme, all-or-nothing terms. You make one mistake and decide you are terrible at everything. You see somebody else succeed and conclude you will never be as good. When you think in black-and-white terms, you deny the possibility of alternatives and remain trapped in a place of low self-esteem. Example: *"My boss made corrections on the assignment I turned in. I am terrible at this job. She hates me and thinks I'm incompetent."*

Have you ever used black or white thinking? Give an example:

_____

_____

_____

Minimization

Minimization occurs when you diminish your accomplishments or underestimate your abilities. People with low self-esteem routinely prevent themselves from taking pride in their successes by discrediting everything they do. Because they believe they are not worthy, they convince themselves that their achievements are insignificant. Example: *"It doesn't matter that I received this award. Anyone could have done what I did. It wasn't that hard."*

Have you ever minimized something that you should have given yourself credit for? Give an example:

_____

_____

_____

Catastrophizing

The flip side to minimization is catastrophizing, where weaknesses are magnified and blown out of proportion. People with low self-esteem overemphasize the importance of flaws and ruminate on mistakes. They view failures as proof that they are not good enough. Example: *"I said something stupid and called that person the wrong name. She probably thinks I'm an idiot. I'm never going to make friends."*

Have you ever blown a situation out of proportion? Give an example:

_____

_____

_____

Personalization

People with low self-esteem tend to feel overly responsible for everything. They take things personally and unnecessarily apologize and self-blame. Example: *"He's not calling me back. Maybe I shouldn't have called him. He probably is ignoring me because he doesn't like me and thinks I'm annoying."*

Have you taken something personally when it wasn't you after all? Explain:

_____

_____

_____

_____

Mind Reading and Jumping to Conclusions

Mind reading and jumping to conclusions happen when you make assumptions about what other people are thinking, when you presume that others are judging you unfavorably, and when you predict negative outcomes for the future. Example: *"Everyone here probably thinks I am weird and annoying. I am never going to fit in."*

Have you ever jumped to an erroneous conclusion? Explain:

_____

_____

_____

_____

Labeling

Labeling happens when you call yourself a mean name. People with low self-esteem are often in the habit of labeling themselves negatively. Even light-hearted criticisms can perpetuate low self-esteem. Example: *"I'm such an idiot. What a loser."*

Have you ever labeled yourself unfairly? Explain:

_____

_____

_____

Are there other ways you engage in negative self-talk?

_____

_____

_____

If you pay attention to the messages your internal voice is telling you, you can classify different types of self-talk into these categories. This will help you to more easily identify any irrational thinking.

Paying attention to your internal voice can be hard at first if you aren't in the habit of really listening to your internal dialogue and bringing your subconscious thoughts into your conscious mind. Make an effort to become more aware of what is going on in your thoughts throughout the day. Writing your thoughts down on paper can help you get into the habit of really listening to what you are thinking by bringing abstract thoughts into concrete, sentence form.

Using the charts on the following pages, identify eight times of the day that are part of your normal routine. For example, waking up, brushing your teeth, eating breakfast, lunch, and dinner, commuting to and from work, and going to bed at night. Write the times you've chosen in the first column, under "Time of Day." On five separate days, work to pay close attention to what is going on in your mind, especially during these distinct times. Write a few sentences that capture what is going on in your internal dialogue.

After you've filled in the charts, go back and look over your responses. What is the general tone of your self-talk? Are you more prone to positive thinking? Or do your thoughts tend to be filled with anxious and self-deprecating messages? Do you see any patterns of thinking, or can you identify any examples of distorted thinking that fall into the categories previously discussed?

For example, the following are five days' worth of Jenny's self-talk during her morning commute to work:

TIME OF DAY	DAY NO.	SELF-TALK SENTENCE
During morning commute	Day 1:	I can't believe I'm late for work. This accident had better clear up soon. I'm going to feel so stupid walking in late to this meeting. My boss is going to be furious.
	Day 2:	I wonder if I should stop and get donuts for the client meeting today. I think I have time, and I'm really hungry. Maybe bagels would be better.
	Day 3:	I'm really nervous about this presentation. I'm scared I'm going to look stupid. I can be such an idiot. I have to stay positive. I know my stuff. I can do it.
	Day 4:	Urgh. It's such a dreary day. It was so hard getting out of bed, and I really don't feel like going to work. I wish I could have just called in sick, but I have that meeting this afternoon.
	Day 5:	I'm really excited about my dinner plans tonight. I can't wait to see my friends.

Some of Jenny's self-talk includes mundane thoughts—whether to stop to pick up breakfast, noting the weather, thinking about her plans for the evening. Yet negative self-talk also creeps in—fear of feeling stupid, assumptions that her boss will be mad, labeling herself as an idiot. At times, Jenny is able to give herself positive, encouraging self-talk, such as, "I can do it."

The goal in this exercise is to get you to start paying attention to what goes on in your mind and to get an overview of the tone of your own self-talk. Eventually you will work to eliminate the negative messaging as much as possible while increasing your positive self-talk.

Monitoring Self-Talk

TIME OF DAY	DAY NO.	SELF-TALK SENTENCE

TIME OF DAY	DAY NO.	SELF-TALK SENTENCE

Personal Pressure

Women with low self-esteem and negative self-talk place great pressure on themselves. The unwinnable quest to be perfect or do the impossible can only disappoint. If this dilemma rings true for you, you may relate to messages about what you should do and who you should be, frequently utilizing "should" statements.

Stop and think about your own personal expectations, plans, and goals, whether short- or long-term. Do you have any messages to yourself that start with "I should," "I have to," or "I need to"? If so, write them here.

_____

_____

_____

_____

The problem with messages that begin with anything like "I should," "I have to," "I need to," and "I must" is that these types of statements create strict absolutes and inflexible demands. They are unrealistic and don't leave room for the setbacks and imperfections that inevitably touch our lives. When we think in uncompromising ways and create rigid expectations for ourselves, we set ourselves up for failure that can lead to more critical self-talk, further depleting self-esteem.

As you get to know yourself better, strive to identify your negative self-talk and pay particular attention to your use of absolutes in your language. In addition to "should" statements, words that convey extremes, like "always" and "never," create similar traps. ("*I always do everything wrong*" and "*I will never be able to accomplish this.*") By eliminating the absolute language from your self-talk, you can protect self-esteem and begin working toward creating a habit of healthier, more productive self-talk. Good substitutions for "should" statements include phrases like, "I could," "I would like to," "I choose to," and "I want to." These phrases set up more realistic and forgiving scenarios that allow you to start being kinder to yourself.

In the space provided, see if you can reframe the following "should" statements to utilize more flexible language, such as "I choose to" or "I would like to":

I have to get an A on this test.

_____

I should lose 20 pounds.

_____

I need to find another job this week.

_____

When I need to be somewhere, I make a point not to think, _"I have to be there by noon."_ Instead, I think, _"I would like to be there on time, right at noon."_ Anything can happen to get in the way of even the best-laid plans. Even if I make every effort to leave early to allow plenty of time, I could run into unavoidable traffic due to a bad accident. If I'm late, it's easier to forgive myself and move on if I told myself I would like to be on time versus if I had said I _had_ to. If I told myself I had to and didn't meet that goal, I would inevitably feel like a failure. If I tell myself I would like to, I may still be disappointed or frustrated, but it's easier to blame the negativity on the obstacles that got in the way rather than on any personal failure.

Even slight shifts in the way you phrase communication can create a world of difference in how you ultimately feel. Learning to identify the specific language in your thinking is a big part of knowing yourself and understanding how your thoughts might create problems with self-esteem. Once you've identified your unhealthy thinking habits, you can make changes that will result in an improvement in self-esteem.

TAYLOR'S STORY

Taylor called me to schedule an appointment for career counseling. Typically, when people come in for career counseling, they are at a loss for where to begin looking for jobs. They need help honing their skills, discovering their passion, and deciding what type of jobs to apply for.

I was prepared to administer career assessments, but within minutes of meeting Taylor, I realized she knew exactly what she wanted to do. She had recently graduated from law school and had just passed the bar exam. She had already been on several interviews at law firms and had more lined up for the following week.

I quickly discovered that Taylor didn't need guidance in figuring out what to do with her life or help with finding a job (she got two offers the following week). Rather, she needed help managing her anxiety, finding balance and patience, and stepping back from the extreme amount of pressure she placed on herself.

The problem was, Taylor's thoughts were filled with "should" statements. "I should have a job by now," "I need to start making money," "I have to get an offer soon," and "I will never be happy if I can't use my law degree." Her standards and expectations for herself were so unrealistic and stringent that she failed to see the positives: that she had earned her degree, had passed the bar, and was landing interviews during a time when it was difficult for recent graduates to find entry-level jobs. She was minimizing, catastrophizing, jumping to conclusions, and thinking in black-and-white terms all at the same time.

As we continued to work together, I learned that Taylor's personal demands also applied to every other aspect of her life. She was a perfectionist in her work, had rigorous expectations about her need to exercise daily, and held unrealistic standards in her dating life. As a result, Taylor frequently felt disappointed with herself, discouraged about her future, and fearful that her job was in jeopardy because she didn't feel good enough.

Becoming more aware of how her rigid and unrealistic patterns of thinking were getting in the way was the first step in Taylor's journey to knowing herself. Once she understood her default pattern, she could begin setting more realistic expectations and work toward improved self-esteem.

Do you identify with anything from Taylor's story?

_____

_____

_____

Do you tend to think in extremes or absolutes? If so, how?

_____

_____

_____

_____

In what areas do you set rigid or strict expectations for yourself?

_____

_____

_____

_____

FEELING VERSUS FACT

As you dig into who you are, get in touch with your inner voice, and explore aspects of your past that contribute to your struggles with self-esteem, it can feel as if your life is a mess. Many women identify with *every* category of distorted thinking and are left feeling like building self-esteem will be a very steep uphill battle. But don't let these feelings discourage you.

While you cannot change your childhood, upbringing, history, or experiences that have led you to where you are today, you *can* change the way you think and feel about various situations and yourself as a result. In future steps, you'll learn ways to implement tools and new behaviors to set these changes into motion. But right now you are doing important work too, just by becoming more aware, identifying what gets in the way of having healthier self-esteem and looking for any learning opportunity in challenges or setbacks. When you find yourself feeling overwhelmed or disappointed, ask yourself what the situation taught you or what strengths you may have taken away from the experience.

MORGAN'S STORY

Morgan was a high school student dealing with depression and anxiety. While she struggled with motivation and keeping commitments in nearly every area of her life, she never missed a therapy session; however, her symptoms did not seem to be improving. She frequently changed the subject when I asked about her feelings, and she seemed indifferent to the tools I tried to teach her, failing to do homework or practice anything she was learning in our sessions.

I finally confronted Morgan, questioning why she continued coming to therapy every week when she seemed so unmotivated to make changes. She broke into tears, saying she had nobody else to talk to, then explained there was something important she needed to deal with but said she hadn't yet found the courage to tell me.

She'd finally broached the fact that she was hiding a secret, but it took another week for her to feel ready to share that when she was 13, she had become involved with a man she had met online. Getting this off her chest was a turning point, and our sessions took on a new direction as we began working through what had happened, processing all of her emotions, including the huge amounts of shame and guilt that she experienced as a result of what she'd been through.

Morgan initially struggled to see the experience as one of abuse, in which she was a victim, groomed by a pedophile. She was certain she was to blame and that what happened was her fault. After all, she had liked the attention in the beginning and enjoyed hearing the nice things he said to her. He made her feel special—until he started asking her to do things that made her feel uncomfortable, dirty, and filled with regret.

Morgan spent the next few years after the experience bearing the burden alone and feeling guilt-ridden, damaged, and hopeless about the possibility of putting the experience behind her. As she learned more about the insidious nature of sexual predators and the effects of trauma and abuse, she became better able to understand what had happened to her. Rather than see herself as a corrupted child looking for trouble, she recognized that she had been a lonely child in need of attention.

She was able to begin letting go of the sense of responsibility that kept her trapped in feelings of depression and worthlessness. Instead, she turned her focus onto the strength it had required to ultimately end the relationship and find the courage to share her experience.

As we ended therapy prior to her going away to college, Morgan reflected on the past several years, saying, "You know, in a way, I'm kind of glad it happened. I mean, not that I was abused or had my innocence stolen from me; but that I had an experience that taught me that I can overcome and rise above anything that comes my way."

Do you identify with anything Morgan was feeling?

_____

_____

_____

_____

Do you struggle with any feelings of shame, guilt, or remorse? If so, what are the feelings, and how do you think they could hold you back from healthy self-esteem?

_____

_____

_____

_____

Do you have any deep secrets or skeletons in your closet that you might need to address in order to move forward toward healthier self-esteem? If so, write about what they are.

_____

_____

_____

_____

WOMEN, SHAME, AND GUILT

Shame and guilt are particularly devastating to women's self-esteem. When self-esteem is low, women tend to personalize everything that happens, feeling guilty and taking responsibility for things that go wrong. Through negative self-talk, the guilt is transformed to shame, resulting in messages that say, "I did something wrong, therefore I am bad, I am flawed, I am worthless." Shame is counterproductive to the development of healthy self-esteem, keeping a woman trapped in intensely painful feelings and beliefs of worthlessness, isolation, and powerlessness.

Shame researcher Brené Brown cites three steps to banishing shame:

1. Talk to yourself like you would talk to someone you love.

2. Reach out to someone you trust.

3. Tell your story, because shame cannot survive being spoken.

Simply put, empathy is the antidote to shame. In being more compassionate in your own self-talk and in telling your story to someone you can trust to provide empathy and validation, you can end the powerful destruction of shame and move toward healthy self-esteem.

Rewriting Your Story

Kids are so smart. When they mess up, they simply say "Do-over!" And they do it over! Well, what's to stop grown-ups from do-overs? We are all works in progress, and if we can see ourselves as such, and use that mind-set to propel us forward with a more positive outlook as we get wiser with every do-over, we can only get better.

As you reflect on the experiences that shaped your current level of self-esteem, see if you can rewrite your story to find the silver lining, lessons, or positive takeaways. You cannot change your history, but you can change the way you feel about past experiences, and you can also control how you talk to yourself about your role in various circumstances. Maybe you were just doing the best you could to survive chaos, confusion, or dysfunction.

Name some aspects of your life that have contributed to low self-esteem:

_____

_____

_____

_____

What coping attempts (healthy or unhealthy) have you used to deal with these experiences?

_____

_____

_____

_____

Looking at your past through a lens of self-compassion, can you identify any ways these experiences made you stronger or taught you invaluable lessons?

_____

_____

_____

_____

Look Back to Move Forward

Before we move on to the next chapter, spend some time thinking about the major points of this step, Know Yourself, and reflect upon what you have learned and how this knowledge has shaped your current view of yourself. Messages we receive or perceive from experiences throughout our lives play a role in our sense of self and how we feel about our individual identity. These experiences also shape the way we think about, talk to, and treat ourselves.

To build self-esteem, we need to identify our internal dialogue and understand how distorted thinking and unrealistic pressures we place on ourselves impede our ability to experience self-worth. While we cannot change the facts of our past, we can work to change our negative self-talk and find meaning that moves us forward toward acceptance and growth.

Write about what you have learned in this chapter and how you can use it to strengthen your self-esteem.

_____

_____

_____

_____

You may be feeling a variety of things after reading this chapter and delving into your past experiences. Write about what you're feeling and consider how you can use these feelings to move forward with building your self-esteem.

_____

_____

_____

_____

TAKE ACTION!

Here are some suggested activities you can do to reinforce what you've learned.

1. Look back at old family photographs and write about what your life was like as a child.
2. Write down three examples of negative self-talk you caught in your internal dialogue this week. See if you can identify the distortions.
3. Come up with three examples of positive self-talk—or even just one. Write them down and consider how they make you feel.
4. Watch Brené Brown's "Listening to shame" TED Talk (available online).
5. Identify a challenge or setback you encountered this week and see if you can pinpoint one positive lesson that came from the experience.

Care for Yourself

CARING FOR YOURSELF IS WELL ESTABLISHED as the path to well-being, but it is less obviously recognized as a critical factor in developing and maintaining healthy self-esteem. Caring for every aspect of your identity is vital to developing a sense of self-worth.

By caring for yourself physically and emotionally, you send yourself and others the message that you are important and worthy. When you fail to care for yourself, you send powerful and damaging signals to yourself that you are unimportant and insignificant. Caring for yourself involves treating yourself well, making healthy choices, and prioritizing your own well-being. In this step, we will look at specific ways you can implement self-care tools that will contribute to developing healthier self-esteem.

Creating a Habit of Caring Self-Talk

As we explored in the previous step, the way we think and our internal voice dictates our feelings and moods and contributes to our level of self-esteem. Once you come to know yourself and can identify the negative patterns in your thinking, the next step is to begin challenging and reframing these thoughts into messages that are more caring and self-nurturing. By taking better care of yourself through the way you think and talk, you can improve self-esteem and live a more fulfilling life.

Changing unproductive patterns in thinking and behavior is the basis of cognitive behavioral therapy, an effective, evidence-based method for treating issues like anxiety and depression and improving overall mental health. Changing negative self-talk is a pretty straightforward concept: replacing the habit of thinking negatively with a healthier practice of thinking in more rational and encouraging ways.

The strategy is simple: When you catch yourself engaging in negative self-talk, stop. Sometimes it can be helpful to use a visual aid, like imagining a big red stop sign or a slamming door anytime you begin to engage in negative or pessimistic thinking. Draw the visual aid you plan to use in the space provided:

Next, see if you can come up with a rational, kind statement to replace the negative message. Your new sentence doesn't have to be the opposite of your negative self-talk; it just needs to be something rational, neutral, and devoid of destructive judgment.

For example, if you find yourself thinking, "*I'm such an idiot. I can't believe I just did that,*" stop! You don't have to think "*I'm so smart,*" but you can simply say, "*Everyone makes mistakes.*" As you can see, these reframes don't necessarily need to be filled with praise; they just need to be realistic messages that refrain from self-condemnation. Let's practice changing negative self-talk by taking a look at some of the examples from the previous chapter. See if you can reframe the statements in the following exercise to include more rational, positive self-talk.

REFRAMING NEGATIVE SELF-TALK

"My boss made corrections on the assignment I turned in. I am terrible at this job. She hates me and thinks I'm incompetent."

Rational Reframe:

_____

_____

_____

_____

"It doesn't matter that I received this award. Anyone could have done what I did. It wasn't that hard."

Rational Reframe:

_____

_____

_____

_____

"I said something stupid and called that person the wrong name. She probably thinks I'm an idiot. I'm never going to make friends."

Rational Reframe:

_____

_____

_____

_____

"He's not calling me back. He probably doesn't like me."

Rational Reframe:

_____

_____

_____

_____

"I'm such an idiot. What a loser."

Rational Reframe:

_____

_____

_____

_____

If you were able to reframe your responses, pat yourself on the back for knowing what it takes to utilize healthy, positive self-talk. If you found it difficult to reframe the statements, don't worry—it can take practice to reprogram old thinking habits. Possible reframes for these statements might look like this:

"My boss made corrections on the assignment I turned in. Looks like there may be a bit of a learning curve."

"I received this award. Good for me!"

"I said something stupid and called that person the wrong name. Urgh. I'm embarrassed, but everyone makes mistakes. It's not the end of the world."

"He's not calling me back. Maybe he's busy."

"I'll be okay."

Of course, it's much easier to reframe hypothetical statements or those made by somebody else when you are just an observer. Initially, it may be harder to do this with your own thought patterns, but, with dedicated effort and lots of practice, you will eventually be able to break the habit of negative self-talk. Remember the research on rewiring the brain (page 41)? The more you practice stopping your negative thoughts and replacing them with more rational, kind messages, the closer you will get to forming healthy habits of thinking positively and establishing healthy self-esteem.

As you notice negative self-talk, begin working to champion an inner voice that is healthy and reassuring. At first, you may sense some internal conflict as you experience what feels like a battle of two different voices in your head—one that is negative, self-deprecating, and determined to keep you stuck, and one that is desperately trying to provide compassion and paint a brighter picture. Sometimes it may feel like those old cartoons that depict a devil on one shoulder and an angel on the other. In time, the negative voice will lessen as you build up your arsenal of positive statements and strengthen your ability to engage in healthy self-talk.

Let's start building that positive arsenal now. Use the following chart. In the first column, write down five negative messages you catch yourself thinking during the course of the next week. In the middle column, reframe them into kinder, more productive statements. Consider how this changes your mood and the way you feel about yourself overall. Note the change in the third column. If you are still struggling to recognize and catch your negative self-talk, it may help to start by identifying your feelings. As previously mentioned, our negative emotions are fueled by negative self-talk. When you find yourself feeling especially upset, stop and try to identify what your inner voice is telling you. Writing and challenging negative self-talk messages on paper will help you really grasp how reframing works. In time, it will become easier to do without having to write the sentences down.

Reframing Your Own Negative Self-Talk

NEGATIVE MESSAGE	RATIONAL REFRAME	OUTCOME
EXAMPLE: I really screwed up. I am such a failure.	Everyone makes mistakes.	I feel less guilty and terrible about myself.

AFFIRMATIONS

Reframing your negative self-talk is an important part of caring for yourself and a vital element to building healthy self-esteem. But more is needed.

Remember how we talked about the mind's predisposition toward the negative? Research looking at the effects of positive and negative comments has demonstrated that it actually takes *multiple* positive comments to counter the effect of just one negative comment, with the ideal ratio being somewhere around five positive comments for every one negative comment! This means that it's not enough just to counter a negative self-talk message with a positive reframe. You also need to feed yourself a constant stream of positive messages that outweigh the years of negative, self-critical commentary.

The way to do this is to begin intentionally adding affirmations into your inner dialogue. Affirmations are positive, encouraging, and upbeat statements that affect our subconscious minds and can truly help influence habits, actions, feelings, and behaviors. Affirmations for caring for yourself and building self-esteem include statements like, *I choose to be well*, *I deserve happiness*, *I am worthy*, *I am good enough*, and *I have value*. Essentially, you are treating yourself like a good friend.

An important part of creating affirmations is to be sure they are written in the first person and in the present tense. This gives them more power. It may be a challenge at first. When your self-esteem is low, it can be hard to accept affirmations as true for yourself, and it can be difficult to say them aloud. I tell people to "fake it until you make it." While it may feel ridiculous to talk to yourself using positive affirmations, try it anyway. The more you practice, the less silly it will feel. If you really struggle with saying anything to the same effect as the examples provided, try adding the bridge phrase "I am learning to"—*I am learning to be well*, *I am learning to feel I deserve happiness*, *I am learning to feel worthy*, *I am learning to feel good enough*, and *I am learning to acknowledge my value*.

In the space provided, create a list of at least 10 affirmations that you can begin using. Write five affirmations regarding things you already feel good about and want to focus on. Write five that address what you WANT to believe about yourself, even if you don't yet feel these things are true. If it feels too early to say, for example, "I'm strong," you can say "*I'm learning to be strong.*"

Make it a point to say them aloud throughout your day. It can be especially helpful to create an affirmations routine or ritual; for example, say them every morning upon waking, at night before you go to bed, while you are in front of the mirror brushing your teeth, or in your car as you are driving. If you need help creating affirmations, search "affirmations" in Google Images, and you will find uplifting examples of affirmations and inspiring quotes to help guide you. Pay particular attention to any affirmations that feel particularly difficult for you to accept, as these likely shed light on areas where you need the most practice.

My Affirmations

1. _____
2. _____
3. _____
4. _____
5. _____
6. _____
7. _____
8. _____
9. _____
10. _____

EMMA'S STORY

When Emma first started therapy, she was struggling with low self-esteem and social anxiety that had become so debilitating she had a difficult time leaving her house. She stopped going to classes, was ready to give up her favorite hobby, and dreaded having to do anything that involved interacting with others, even ordering food or making phone calls.

When I taught her about affirmations, I could tell she thought it sounded completely crazy. I knew there was no way she would go home and formulate and practice her own affirmations without a greater push in that direction. So, I pulled out a pad of sticky notes and decided that we were going to create a handful of affirmations together. Coming up with her own affirmations was at first a challenge. She sat silently and shrugged her shoulders when I asked what she thought I should write; however, when I started to make some suggestions, she was able to tweak the wording into sentences she felt she could actually try to say.

We wrote down 10 affirmations, and she took them home with the instruction to place them around the house, in places where she would regularly see them. She put them in her wallet, next to her bed, and on her mirror, car dashboard, refrigerator, and cabinets. Every time she saw an affirmation, she was to read it aloud.

At her next session, Emma reported it was initially difficult to believe the words she was saying. She felt silly and like a complete liar telling herself things like, "I am awesome," "I am talented," and "I can do anything." But she pushed through the discomfort and continued to repeat them, multiple times every day.

Soon, she memorized the words on the paper and challenged herself to remember each affirmation as she was falling asleep at night. In time, Emma recited the affirmations with ease, began to add new ones to her list, and consequently experienced a decrease in her anxiety as a result of committing to the practice of using affirmations as a tool. When she felt nervous or insecure, Emma repeated, "I've got this," "I can do it," and "I'm perfectly fine" to herself over and over and discovered it really did give her the courage to do things she had previously avoided.

Does your self-esteem cause you to avoid social interactions? If so, in what ways?

_____

_____

_____

_____

Do you feel skeptical about self-help tools and their ability to alter aspects of your life? If so, which ones and why?

_____

_____

_____

_____

Can you recall any times where you took a chance on something that ended up being helpful?

_____

_____

_____

_____

Even if you initially feel skeptical or awkward about using affirmations, give them a chance. You will likely find that they become easier with practice.

Banishing Self-Doubt

As you begin putting these tools into practice, you may hear the voice of self-doubt creeping in, trying to make you believe you aren't capable of change or suggesting that this work is too hard to bother trying. Therefore, part of this step involves eliminating any self-doubt that stands in your way.

Do you tend to struggle with feelings of self-doubt? Answer the following questions to find out.

1. I have difficulty sharing my opinions and ideas.   TRUE   FALSE

2. I find it hard to speak up.   TRUE   FALSE

3. I avoid taking risks.   TRUE   FALSE

4. I frequently fear judgment by others.   TRUE   FALSE

5. I have difficulty taking credit.	TRUE	FALSE
6. I frequently apologize, even when something is not my fault.	TRUE	FALSE
7. I have difficulty making decisions.	TRUE	FALSE
8. I often procrastinate.	TRUE	FALSE
9. I have a hard time accepting compliments.	TRUE	FALSE
10. I find it hard to make eye contact with others.	TRUE	FALSE
11. I tend to give unnecessary or excessive explanations.	TRUE	FALSE
12. I often make self-deprecating jokes.	TRUE	FALSE
13. I engage in nervous habits, like anxious laughter or nail biting.	TRUE	FALSE
14. I have a hard time requesting and receiving help.	TRUE	FALSE

If you answered "true" to many of these statements, you likely deal with feelings of self-doubt that will test your confidence and motivation as you work through the steps to building self-esteem. Fear and hesitation created by self-doubt impede our ability to take risks that move us toward growth and change. Self-doubt creates anxiety, which leads to procrastination, wasted mental energy, an inability to concentrate, and an ultimate tendency to self-sabotage.

The key to banishing self-doubt is to rise above the reservations and find the courage to take small, manageable steps in a new direction. Building healthy self-esteem is a life changer, but the fundamentals of getting there are pretty simple. Utilize healthy self-talk and speak to yourself the way you would talk to a close friend, encouraging yourself forward. As you consciously stop focusing on the negatives and replace them with hopeful affirmations, you open yourself to believing you are good and capable. This new mind-set will allow you to develop confidence in your abilities, trust in your instincts, and self-assurance that you can effectively handle anything that comes your way.

Write down two encouraging statements that you would say to a friend who is struggling:

1. _____

2. _____

Now practice saying those same sentences to yourself.

Your Health

Caring for yourself includes taking care of both your physical and mental health. The basic things people think about when they consider health and well-being, like exercise, eating well, getting enough rest, and managing stress, are all important areas to consider when striving to build self-esteem. Our sense of self-worth is directly correlated to the priority we place on our physical and emotional health.

In line with the adage "actions speak louder than words," our actions can communicate powerful messages that ultimately contribute to levels of self-esteem. When you pay attention to your health and make choices that are in line with a healthy lifestyle, you are telling yourself that you are important and worthwhile. Look at the items on the following list, and check off anything you are prone to doing:

☐ Overworking or pushing myself too hard
☐ Overeating
☐ Restricting eating
☐ Exercising too hard
☐ Avoiding exercise
☐ Overindulging
☐ Overspending
☐ Ignoring my feelings
☐ Ignoring my intuition
☐ Faking happiness around others

Women with low self-esteem tend to sacrifice their own needs and attention to self-care. They also are likely to engage in unhealthy behaviors when stressed, putting their health on the back burner due to not feeling good or deserving enough, which ultimately feeds into the reinforcement of low self-esteem. If you can relate to this, you can benefit from spending some time considering what your current level of self-care looks like and where you can make improvements.

Caring for Your Physical Health

There are three major components to caring for your physical health: eating well, exercising regularly, and getting enough restful sleep. As you work on these areas, be sure to seek out the help of professionals when needed and keep on top of things like medical appointments to ensure your overall physical well-being.

EATING

What you put into your body sends important messages about how much you value yourself and prioritize leading a healthy life. This subject can fill a book on its own. Essentially, you'll want to consider your current eating habits and strive to make changes to consciously eat right. This includes eating balanced, regularly scheduled meals, including foods that are healthy and nutritious, eating in moderation, listening to your body signals and hunger cues regarding when you are hungry or full, and avoiding pitfalls like emotional eating or fad diets that set the stage for failure. If you struggle with eating issues, seek out the help of your health care provider or better yet, a qualified nutritionist, who can help you find balance in this area.

EXERCISING

Look at your relationship with exercise and think about what physical activities you currently do and for what reasons. Exercise also plays a role in our level of self-esteem. Did you know that exercise releases hormones that create the same neurological effects as antidepressant medication? Exercise can be highly effective in decreasing depressive moods that can aggravate low self-esteem. I can't emphasize this enough: Make some form of physical activity a regular part of your life. Standing is better than sitting; five minutes spent moving is better than nothing—the point is, every bit helps. Seek out activities and routines that allow you to stay consistent and find enjoyment, with enough variety to stay interested.

SLEEPING

Your body does important work while you sleep—this is when it restores and repairs itself! To feel at your best, ensure you are consistently getting enough restful sleep. Poor sleep can leave you feeling irritable and thus more vulnerable to the anxious and negative self-talk messages that chip away at self-esteem. If sleep is an issue for you, it can be helpful to create a structured routine around bedtime. Turn off electronics an hour or two before bed, drink some chamomile tea, and spray a little lavender on your pillow. Instead of falling asleep to the television, offer yourself gentler options like a light read or a meditation.

Next, we will explore goal setting in the areas of diet, exercise, and rest. As you move through these different areas, be realistic with your expectations. Pay close attention to the language you use as you set your goals and plans for creating a healthier lifestyle. Remember to continue paying attention to self-talk and watch out for those meddlesome "should" statements that will set you up for failure rather than encourage you to move forward in your journey. We will begin by showing you how to set small goals you can build upon, rather than lofty ones that may set you up for disappointment if not achieved.

Let's explore your experience with goal setting:

Can you identify a time you set unrealistic goals and didn't make much progress?

_____

_____

_____

_____

What could you have done differently to ensure greater success?

_____

_____

_____

_____

Can you identify a time when you set appropriate goals? What was the result?

_____

_____

_____

_____

Reflect upon your motivation in setting various goals, especially as they relate to your body image and appearance. The attention you give your physical appearance directly relates to your self-talk and its correlation to your self-esteem. Does the desire to achieve a certain body type or look a certain way come from a place of wanting to feel strong and healthy because you feel worthy and deserving? Or does it come from an obsession with trying to achieve perfection, keep up with what you see in others, or gain external validation because you don't currently feel at peace with your body image?

I am motivated by:

_____

_____

_____

_____

A healthy body image doesn't mean you look like a model; rather, it means you are generally content with your body the way it is, and you accept that you have positive qualities as well as flaws. Women with a healthy body image appreciate their bodies for what they do rather than how they look, and recognize that there are greater measures of worth than appearance.

List three things you can appreciate about what your body does for you:

1. _____
2. _____
3. _____

List three things about your body that you like or are content with:

1. _____
2. _____
3. _____

It's perfectly fine to care about appearance—to want to stay fit, to enjoy dressing and looking nice, and to choose to use makeup and hair products to look your best—but pay particular attention to self-talk around motivation to achieve these things. Are you sending yourself any rigid messages or basing your worth on your ability to live up to unrealistic standards? Or are you able to view body image and appearance as only one aspect of who you are?

A focus on appearance can be healthy when we're motivated by the right things. When we put effort into taking care of our bodies and looking our best, we send ourselves powerful messages about our self-value. If the energy we put into appearance comes from a place of healthy goals and a desire to feel good, great. If, however, it comes from distorted messages or rigid expectations, we do ourselves more harm than good.

We can all stand to improve our body language. Our posture and the way we carry ourselves influence how we feel and look. This is an easy quick fix that you can do anytime—at work, at home, or even while you're standing in a line:

- Stand purposefully, with your hips evenly aligned over your legs
- Drop your arms to your sides and breathe deeply
- Stand up straight, pulling your shoulders back
- Lift your chin and relax into a gentle smile
- Speak clearly, using good eye contact

Congrats—no matter how uncertain you feel on the inside, you just presented yourself with confidence!

EVALUATING AND SETTING EXPECTATIONS FOR PHYSICAL HEALTH

Evaluate the following areas of your physical health and check whether you feel satisfied with each category. If not, consider what your goals for change might be, then check to see whether they are realistic and achievable, staying away from anything too inflexible or idealistic. Rework your goals until you can check the box confirming they are realistic and achievable.

My current eating habits:

_____

_____

_____

_____

☐ I am satisfied with my eating habits.
☐ I am not happy with my eating habits.

Goals for improved eating habits:

_____

_____

_____

_____

☐ These goals are realistic and achievable.

My current physical exercise habits:

_____

_____

_____

_____

☐ I am satisfied with my exercise habits.
☐ I am not happy with my exercise habits.

Goals for improved exercise habits:

_____

_____

_____

_____

☐ These goals are realistic and achievable.

My current sleep habits:

_____

_____

_____

_____

☐ I am satisfied with my sleep habits.
☐ I am not happy with my sleep habits.

Goals for improved sleep habits:

_____

_____

_____

_____

☐ These goals are realistic and achievable.

My appearance and body image:

_____

_____

_____

_____

☐ I am satisfied with my appearance and body image.
☐ I am not happy with my appearance and body image.

Goals for improved appearance and body image:

_____

_____

_____

_____

☐ These goals are realistic and achievable.

Caring for Your Mental Health

Taking care of your mental health is another vital component in working toward improved self-esteem. Low self-esteem goes hand in hand with a number of mental health issues, including depression, anxiety, stress, PTSD, addiction, abuse, and relationship dissatisfaction. Your ability to engage in these steps, especially monitoring self-talk and evaluating satisfaction with various aspects of your life, involves addressing these coexisting mental health concerns and maintaining a calm, focused, and self-aware mind. If your experience includes any of these issues, seek the guidance of a mental health professional who can help you work through these steps while also addressing these other struggles.

Besides low self-esteem, list any additional mental health issues you struggle with:

_____

_____

_____

_____

What would you like to improve with regard to your mental health?

_____

_____

_____

_____

SELF-CARE ACTIVITIES

Mental clarity and emotional stability necessitate taking time out for yourself in order to relax, re-energize, and participate in self-nurturing activities. When your self-esteem is low, you may falsely believe that you aren't worthy of indulging in the things you enjoy. You may tell yourself you don't deserve time out for yourself or that your needs and wishes aren't a priority compared to those of others. However, by denying yourself attention to your own needs, you reinforce feelings and beliefs associated with low self-esteem.

When you take time out to do nice things for yourself and engage in self-nurturing activities you enjoy, this sends the message that you are important and deserving of good things. When you establish more balance between caring for others and engaging in self-care, you create a dynamic that is ultimately healthier for everyone involved! Self-care allows you to recharge your battery. In doing so, you become more available for others and model health and self-esteem to yourself and those around you.

When you think about the concept of self-care, what types of activities come to mind?

_____

_____

_____

_____

_____

Self-care activities can range from simple and free (taking a walk, taking a bubble bath, practicing deep-breathing exercises) to the extravagant (splurging on a great meal, spending a day at the spa, going on vacation). It really doesn't matter what you do for self-care, as long as you make the conscious effort to do *something* regularly with the conscious intention to nurture yourself.

When you choose self-care activities, it's best to maintain some variety so you have many things to choose from when deciding how to spend your time. Some days you may only have two minutes to spare, and that's fine. Other days you may have hours to devote to yourself. Self-care activities can really be anything you enjoy or find relaxing. A handful of examples include:

- Going for a run
- Playing a sport
- Taking a bubble bath
- Making art
- Journaling
- Creative outlets
- Mindfulness/meditation/relaxation techniques
- Volunteering
- Spending time with friends
- Listening to music
- Getting a pedicure

Really, anything you enjoy can be a self-care activity. In the spaces provided, make a list of at least 10 things you can turn to as self-care activities.

My Self-Care Activities

1. _____
2. _____
3. _____
4. _____
5. _____
6. _____
7. _____
8. _____
9. _____
10. _____

CARLA'S STORY

Carla was a busy mom to three busy kids, had a part-time job, and had per-fectionist standards regarding her ability to manage her family, home, and lifestyle. Over the years, Carla's high expectations for herself and tendency to put self-care on the back burner took a toll on her self-esteem.

Learning about the importance of self-care as a necessary component to her goals of improving self-esteem seemed to take a huge weight off Carla's shoulders. Having a sense of permission to take time out for herself was exactly what Carla needed to get back in touch with who she was and provide that foundation for self-awareness and self-esteem.

The next week, Carla came in excited to share that she'd created what she called a Self-Care Coping Box. She'd purchased an index card file box and filled it with color-coded index cards containing different self-care activities—blue for activities that only took a few minutes, like listening to a favorite song, reading a page of an inspirational book, or stepping outside for a breath of fresh air; green for activities that were easy but took more time, like reading a book, watching a movie, or going to yoga; pink for more indulgent activities, like getting her nails done, going out to dinner, or buying a new dress; and yellow for more long-term, extravagant self-care goals like taking a vacation, buying a new car, or having her kitchen remodeled.

Carla made a point each day to select one card from the box, based on the amount of time she could devote to self-care and what she was in the mood for. She said that writing the cards helped her to get back in touch with who she was by thinking about her favorite activities and some of her dreams. Although she didn't plan to spend the money on anything from her yellow cards yet, she liked knowing she had long-term goals and wishes to look forward to. When she felt in the mood to indulge her fantasies, she'd choose a yellow card and allow herself to spend some time surfing Pinterest for the ideal vacation spot or kitchen of her dreams.

Over the course of the next few weeks, Carla continued finding ways to implement and expand her ideas for self-care. She created a place in her house that she called her Self-Care Corner, a little space where she put a bench, some decorative pillows she'd purchased, and a soft blanket. Under the bench she placed a basket filled with scented candles, relaxation CDs, an adult coloring book with colored pencils, and a sound machine that played sounds of raindrops or the ocean.

Carla loved having a space in her house filled with self-care items that she could go to when she felt overwhelmed or stressed. She practiced taking five minutes every day to sit down and use something in her basket to relax. Eventually, just walking past her special space caused her to pause and take a deeper breath before going on with her day.

Carla seemed happier and more confident after she decided to incorporate self-care into her life. Soon, she reported she no longer needed the file box to help her implement self-care. She still looked through it regularly to ensure she wasn't letting any valued pastimes fall by the wayside. However, it was clear that she had shifted her lifestyle to one that included regular self-care, and her self-esteem improved as a result.

Do you ever find yourself overwhelmed, overworked, or overextended like Carla initially felt? Describe how you feel.

_____

_____

_____

_____

Can you identify any things you have done to help relieve your own levels of stress? What works for you?

_____

_____

_____

_____

Do any ideas from Carla's story sound like ones that you might like to try for yourself?

_____

_____

_____

_____

What items would you put in your own self-care box or self-care corner?

_____

_____

_____

_____

MAINTAINING SUPPORTIVE CONNECTIONS

Maintaining a supportive network of people you can depend on can help lead to self-care and strong mental health. Having connections with supportive people—whether family, friends, a mentor, or a trusted therapist—is vital to both well-being and self-esteem. Maslow's hierarchy of needs depicts five levels of needs universal to all humans. After the basics of survival—breathing, food, water, sleep, and safety—comes the intrinsic need we all have for love and belonging. In order to experience emotional well-being, we need to have friendship, intimacy, and a sense of acceptance. Feelings of loneliness, isolation, and abandonment are toxic to self-esteem.

Use the following diagram to map out your various relationships and connections. Inside the blue "micro" circle, write down the names of your closest connections. In the yellow "meso" circle, add any other important relationships, connections, or communities. In the orange "macro" circle, add names of other affiliations or networks that are more on the periphery of your life. You can write a mix of names of individual people and names of institutions or groups. When brainstorming networks and connections that are important to you, consider family members, friends, peers, coworkers, clubs, activities, sports teams, religious affiliations, political parties, your town, state, and so on.

With healthy self-esteem, it's easier to identify the important relationships and components in your network. You are able to keep supportive, encouraging, and uplifting people and experiences in your micro network, while keeping toxic, unhealthy, or more demanding relationships on the periphery. As you work toward building healthier self-esteem, pay attention to the various relationships you identified in your network. Think about who makes you happy and builds you up. Think about who and what depletes your energy or brings you down.

The ideal goal is to maintain at least a handful of very close connections in your micro network. Whether they're family members, close friends, or trusted mentors, these are the people who appreciate you and have your best interest at heart. These are the people you can rely on when you need extra help and support. If you don't have good connections in your network, consider making efforts to meet new people by pursuing new activities or joining new organizations. We will explore relationships and setting boundaries more in future steps.

What are some ways you can expand your network of support? Which of these ideas appeal most to you?

_____

_____

_____

_____

Look Back to Move Forward

Before moving on to the next step, let's look back at what you have learned in this step. Caring for yourself is a vital step toward building self-esteem. Even if you are adept at caring for others, it is the way you care for yourself and prioritize your own needs that plays such an important role in healthy self-esteem.

As you move forward:

Purge the negativity. Continue to practice catching negative self-talk and work to reframe any self-deprecating messages into rational statements that reinforce your value.

Utilize affirmations. Give yourself praise and encouragement. Be your own cheerleader and create rituals and routines that incorporate affirmations on a daily basis. You'll reprogram your brain as a result of the practice that goes into establishing this new habit.

Beware of self-doubt. Take small risks and challenge yourself to try new things. Remember that building self-esteem takes a series of baby steps. Sometimes it may feel like two steps forward, one step back as you work to banish your inner critic and feel deserving of good, but keep pushing forward.

 ## THE OXYGEN MASK THEORY

Women generally assume the role of caretaker, tending to the needs of children, significant others, and elderly parents. They are typically the ones charged with handling additional family responsibilities, such as maintaining friendships and nurturing relationships by remembering birthdays, shopping for holiday gifts, and acknowledging teachers. With so many responsibilities on their plates, women have a tendency to push their own needs aside.

The problem is, managing all of these things at the expense of your need for downtime negatively impacts self-esteem and sets you up to be taken advantage of or taken for granted. You send the message to yourself and others that you're the caregiver; not the other way around, reinforcing false internal messages that you are unimportant and undeserving of care. Let it not be forgotten that a vital part of building self-esteem involves remembering to prioritize your own self-care.

The popular analogy of the oxygen mask can help you be mindful of the importance of self-care: Every airplane is equipped with oxygen masks that are released in the event of an emergency. Flight attendants instruct passengers to put on and secure their own oxygen masks before helping others. If you forget your own oxygen mask, you could run out of oxygen and be unable to help anyone else.

The same concept is true with caring for yourself. If you put all your effort and energy into caring for everyone else at the expense of your own self-care, you run the risk of burning out. Caring for yourself involves taking time out to nurture your own identity and being willing to ask for and accept support.

Adopt self-care basics. Pay attention to healthy eating, exercise, and sleep, and consider what the motivating factors are as you set realistic goals. Work to find balance and establish a sense of well-being by taking time out every day for self-care.

Build your village. Maintain a network of healthy connections and a strong support system, and limit your time with people who drain your energy or bring you down. Read about "the oxygen mask" (opposite page): Taking care of yourself is not only vital to your self-esteem, it's a gift you give to others.

Write about what you have learned in this chapter and how you can use it to strengthen your self-esteem.

_____

_____

_____

_____

Write about what you're feeling after exploring aspects of your own health and self-care, and consider how you can use this information to move forward with building self-esteem.

_____

_____

_____

_____

TAKE ACTION!

1. On a piece of paper or poster board, create a "vision board"—a collage of affirmative words and quotes from magazine clippings (Google "vision board" for examples).
2. Inspire healthy eating habits by finding five new and healthy recipes.
3. Choose one new exercise activity and try it at least two times during the next month—I especially encourage yoga, which is wonderful for the mind-body connection!

4. Write down one simple self-care activity that you can commit to doing at least three times a week. After a week or two, reflect on how having a self-care routine is making you feel.

5. Spend time this week with someone who makes you happy.

• • • • •

Respect Yourself

KNOWING WHO YOU ARE AND CARING for yourself are the fundamental steps in developing the necessary understanding and self-compassion to reclaim feelings of self-worth. However, you can't truly develop and maintain healthy self-esteem until you can consistently respect yourself. While self-esteem involves how you think and feel, self-respect is about your actions. How you act and interact with others and the choices you make relate to your level of self-respect and ultimately play a role in your view of self-worth. Self-respect, along with a determination to begin making healthier choices, will help you make the most of the tools provided in previous steps.

Women who make destructive or self-deprecating decisions that demonstrate a lack of self-respect stay trapped in a cycle of low self-esteem. When you fail to make healthy changes, act in self-denying ways, or make poor choices, this inevitably leads to negative self-talk that further depletes self-esteem. In this case, you have to work twice as hard to block negative messages as you find a way to rationalize your actions, inactions, or self-destructive decisions. When you make bad decisions that harm yourself or others, you feel bad about who you are and feel out of control, making healthy self-esteem very difficult.

Can you think of any bad decisions you've made or regrets you have? If so, write about them.

_____

_____

_____

_____

What could you have done differently?

_____

_____

_____

_____

While it may be difficult to reflect on past choices (especially if you regret them!), considering past behaviors is a helpful first step to building up self-respect. Based on these reflections, you can determine your core values and then maintain the discipline (and self-respect!) necessary to ensure that your values stay in line. Learning how to respect yourself also involves looking at ways you honor or discredit yourself. Think of it this way: When we make choices and act in ways that are aligned with healthy values and self-nurturing goals, we feel good about ourselves and are better able to build and maintain self-esteem.

Assessing Your Values

Read the following list of values typically associated with respect, positive self-esteem, and a healthy life. Check the boxes next to the traits that are important to you.

☐ Kindness   ☐ Loyalty   ☐ Balance
☐ Compassion   ☐ Fairness   ☐ Determination
☐ Patience   ☐ Authenticity   ☐ Openness
☐ Honesty   ☐ Humility   ☐ Optimism
☐ Trustworthiness ☐ Peace   ☐ Happiness

Of the values you identified as important to you, choose the three that you see as the most important:

1. _____
2. _____
3. _____

Now list one way you could practice upholding each of those values to demonstrate respect for yourself:

1. _____
2. _____
3. _____

List one way you could convey to others your expectation that they uphold these values in their dealings with you.

_____
_____
_____
_____

Note any difficulties you've had regarding putting these ideas into practice in the past.

_____
_____
_____
_____

Quashing the Need to Please

As you look over the list of values you selected as important to you, reflect upon this: How often do you pursue goals aligned with these values for your own life? And do you expect others to demonstrate these values in their interactions with you to the same extent you demonstrate them toward others? I know it's tricky, but one of the consequences of low self-esteem is that we often work hard to uphold these values in our interactions with others, sometimes sacrificing our own wishes and needs as we deny ourselves the same level of respect in return. This tendency is caused by the approval-seeking that is characteristic of low self-esteem.

Think about how often you defer to others, perhaps allowing them to make choices and decisions for you. Over time, this can result in you losing sight of your identity and straying from your own individual path as you submit to becoming a follower of others. Do you ever agree to things you know you don't want to do or put aside your own wishes and endeavors in order to go along with or assist others? If so, write about the times this has happened:

_____

_____

_____

_____

What prevents you from saying no or making yourself the priority?

_____

_____

_____

_____

You may fear that acting in your own best interest or speaking up will lead to conflict, including judgment, anger, or hurt feelings of others, or may create vulnerability, opening you up to potentially appear selfish or ignorant. Do you ever hesitate to say no to things and wind up overextending yourself? Distorted thinking and fear also leads to people-pleasing behaviors. Fear of failure, disappointing others, or being criticized or rejected gets in the way of making healthy choices that foster individual well-being.

The problem is, giving away your power and diminishing your value by failing to extend the same respect and attention toward your own needs results in more distorted thinking around your worth. Also, attempting to gain worth or significance from pleasing others can also lead to burnout or feelings of resentment or devastation when your help and sacrifices aren't appreciated. Does this sound like something you can relate to? Complete the following assessment to determine where you stand with regard to people-pleasing. As you do so, consider all of your relationships, including those with family, friends, coworkers, and even strangers.

PEOPLE-PLEASING SELF-ASSESSMENT

On a scale of 1 to 5 (1 being "not at all" and 5 being "all the time"), rate how often you engage in the following behaviors:

1. **I say yes when I want to say no.**

1	2	3	4	5
NOT AT ALL	RARELY	SOMETIMES	OFTEN	ALL THE TIME

2. **I take on responsibilities even when I don't really want to.**

1	2	3	4	5
NOT AT ALL	RARELY	SOMETIMES	OFTEN	ALL THE TIME

3. **I feel I have to profusely apologize or make excuses when I cannot say yes to someone.**

1	2	3	4	5
NOT AT ALL	RARELY	SOMETIMES	OFTEN	ALL THE TIME

4. **I feel responsible for other people's feelings.**

1	2	3	4	5
NOT AT ALL	RARELY	SOMETIMES	OFTEN	ALL THE TIME

5. **I keep my thoughts and opinions to myself if they are different than those of others.**

1	2	3	4	5
NOT AT ALL	RARELY	SOMETIMES	OFTEN	ALL THE TIME

6. **I feel very upset if someone is mad at me or doesn't like me.**

1	2	3	4	5
NOT AT ALL	RARELY	SOMETIMES	OFTEN	ALL THE TIME

7. **I have a hard time admitting to others that they have hurt my feelings or upset me.**

1	2	3	4	5
NOT AT ALL	RARELY	SOMETIMES	OFTEN	ALL THE TIME

8. **I go to great lengths to avoid conflict.**

1	2	3	4	5
NOT AT ALL	RARELY	SOMETIMES	OFTEN	ALL THE TIME

Scoring

Add up your score using the following point system:

1 point for every time you marked 1 **Not at all**

2 points for every time you marked 2 **Rarely**

3 points for every time you marked 3 **Sometimes**

4 points for every time you marked 4 **Often**

5 points for every time you marked 5 **All the time**

If you scored above 20 points, you likely struggle with people-pleasing. You will benefit from dedicating time and effort in the following areas:

- Recognizing your own needs
- Taking time for yourself
- Developing and utilizing assertiveness skills (page 138)
- Setting healthy boundaries (page 187)

Think about what drives this need to please. Where does your tendency to accommodate others or put their needs first come from? Reflect on your experiences in life, especially regarding gender roles, as you were growing up. Were there any messages conveyed about your role as a female? Write about what comes to mind:

_____

_____

_____

_____

As you work to break the pattern of people-pleasing, start paying attention to your own needs and make yourself more of a priority. You can begin evening out the playing field in your relationships and interactions with others as you work to establish a greater level of self-respect. Write down times you successfully advocated for your own best interest:

_____

_____

_____

_____

While it is important to respect others, it's equally important to avoid constantly sacrificing your own needs in order to avoid conflict or pacify others. The goal is to create more equality in relationships and to end the cycle of denying your rights and your worth. As you move forward, pay attention to your self-talk in this area and watch out for any distorted beliefs that force you to assume you are obligated to meet everyone else's needs at the expense of your own. You have the right to your own happiness, safety, and emotional well-being.

Write a promise to yourself to gently say no the next time you feel pressured into an obligation. Be as specific as you want (for example: *The next time Jane asks me to watch her son, I'm going to tell the truth and say "I can't help you today, Jane. I am working on a project and won't be able to give your son the attention he deserves.")*

_____

_____

_____

_____

Developing Assertiveness

After years of being a people-pleaser and sacrificing your own needs in favor of others', it can be difficult to make changes. As you learn to value your rights, needs, and the importance of making yourself a priority, it can help to equip yourself with some tools to support this endeavor—you are essentially learning a new language—the language of saying "No, thank you!" As always, continue monitoring self-talk and working to change any distorted thinking that prevents you from speaking up or protecting yourself from things you do not want to take on. Watch out for that destructive internal critic telling you that you are not worthy or deserving of respect. This simply is not true. Seeking to obtain mutual respect in relationships creates equality that everyone benefits from.

Women with people-pleasing tendencies and low self-esteem often act in passive ways, so learning and developing assertiveness tools will be an important part of your journey. Contrary to what you may think, assertiveness is not an inborn trait or a characteristic possible only for naturally confident people. Rather, it's a skill that can be learned, practiced, and cultivated to help you navigate all kinds of situations and ultimately foster better self-respect.

Think about somebody who you admire for her ability to be assertive. What do you notice about that person? How would you assess her level of self-esteem?

_____

_____

_____

_____

Assertiveness involves the ability to express your opinions, preferences, needs, limits, and boundaries in a respectful, polite way. Assertiveness is not the same as aggression, which includes force, threats, and hostility. Assertiveness is an art and a gift—it involves communication that is direct, honest, and firm, yet respectful and aimed at creating harmony in relationships, rather than engaging in power struggles or a need for control. Read on to learn more about it.

ASSESSING YOUR ABILITY TO BE ASSERTIVE

The following scenarios provide examples of three different methods of responding to various situations, including passive (people-pleasing), aggressive, and assertive ways. Circle the letter that corresponds to the option most similar to how you would handle each situation.

1. You loan a friend your sweater and she returns it with a hole in it. How do you respond?

   a. Throw the sweater in the trash and don't mention it.
   b. Scream at the friend, saying, "I cannot believe you are so careless! How could you ruin my sweater and not tell me?"
   c. Calmly say to your friend, "I'm upset that there is a hole in my sweater. I'd like you to be more careful if you are going to continue to borrow my stuff."

2. Your cousin frequently stops by your house uninvited. Tonight she stops by wanting to talk, but you were just about to head out to meet some friends for dinner. How do you respond?

   a. Text your friends, telling them to order without you. You'll be late, if you make it at all.
   b. Flip out on your cousin, saying, "I can't deal with you always stopping by unannounced! I have plans tonight, and I can't help you with your issues."
   c. Tell your cousin, "I really want to listen, but I have plans to meet friends and I really need to leave now. Why don't you call me tomorrow and we can figure out a time that is convenient for both of us?"

3. You take your car in for an oil change. When you pick it up, you are surprised to find they also rotated the tires and replaced the windshield wipers and brake pads without first obtaining your approval. The bill is much more than you were expecting to pay. How do you handle it?

   a. Silently hand over your credit card, feeling sick to your stomach about the unexpected cost.
   b. Shout at the cashier, saying, "This is ridiculous! I did not agree to all these extra services. I refuse to pay, and I'm never bringing my car here again!"
   c. Ask to speak to a manager, and respectfully explain you were not expecting to pay for services you were not aware were being performed. Ask for a mutually agreeable solution; perhaps a discount off the labor or a credit toward future oil changes.

4. You go to a restaurant and order a salad with chicken. When your meal comes, you discover it has shrimp, not chicken. How do you react?

   a. Profusely apologize to the waiter, saying, "I'm so sorry, but I meant to ask for chicken. I'm really sorry to bother you, but I'm actually allergic to shrimp, otherwise I wouldn't mind. Would it be possible to get another salad with chicken instead? I'm so sorry!"
   b. Act annoyed at the server, exclaiming, "You put in the wrong order! I asked for *chicken*, not shrimp! You need to correct this right away!"
   c. Say to the waiter, "I ordered chicken, not shrimp. Would you please get me another salad with chicken?"

In these examples, the assertive responses are indicated in option C. As you look back over the choices you identified with, think about whether you tend to dismiss your own feelings and needs when handling conflict.

Do you find it difficult to be assertive? If so, why?

_____

_____

_____

_____

What causes you to be passive or aggressive versus assertive?

_____

_____

_____

_____

Do you ever over-apologize? If so, why? Can you give examples?

_____

_____

_____

_____

Do you ever find yourself lashing out when feelings of resentfulness and anger build? If so, give examples:

_____

_____

_____

_____

Can you identify any distorted logic in your answers to these questions?

_____

_____

_____

_____

It may be reassuring to know that you can develop assertiveness. Some strategies to hone your ability to act assertively include:

Reframing distorted thinking. When you reflect on situations, stop and look at what may have held you back from being assertive. Consider "what would have been a better response?"

Creating affirmations. These affirmations can be designed specifically to support assertiveness—"I am learning to speak my mind," "I am able to handle conflict with confidence and ease," and "I have the right to my thoughts and opinions."

Practice. Whether you choose to role-play with a friend or practice in front of the mirror, spend time acting out responses to different situations. Practice speaking with a confident voice and a calm body.

ANGIE'S STORY

Angie was a classic people-pleaser. For years, she said yes to everything that was asked of her, despite the fact that this frequently left her feeling over-whelmed and annoyed. Angie struggled with low self-esteem and falsely believed that the credit, validation, and approval she received externally would eventually help her find self-worth. Instead, Angie's inability to be honest about her limits and to protect her own time and resources left her feeling weak and insignificant.

Angie was always the first person her friend, Alexandra, turned to when she needed help with the fund-raisers she frequently spearheaded. Afraid to let her friend down, Angie always agreed. In her family, Angie was the person everyone went to when they had problems or needed advice. Not wanting to appear uncaring, Angie always put aside what she was doing to step in and help. She was also regularly asked to take on additional assignments at work. Rather than feeling confident in her abilities and in her boss's trust of her, Angie felt taken advantage of and used. She didn't know how to tell him that she had too much on her plate and that she frequently took work home, working late into the evening.

To everyone around her, Angie seemed capable, laid back, and happily available. But on the inside, her resentment and feelings of exhaustion were beginning to build. She came to sessions complaining that her coworkers didn't seem to appreciate everything she was doing and ranted about her family's inability to handle anything without her. When a longtime friend, Paul, stopped hanging out with her due to his new girlfriend's jealousy and insecurity over his friendship with another female, Angie became enraged. Although she told Paul she understood, she let her rage out in sessions, fuming, "How could he just ditch me like that? How does he not see how ridiculous this girl is?"

Angie's long-term habits of bottling up her own feelings, suppressing her thoughts, and saying yes to people even when she wanted to say no were starting to take a toll. Rather than feel worthy for her availability and helpfulness to others, she felt defeated, overwhelmed, and miserable.

We began working on assertiveness training; first, by exploring what made it difficult for her to be honest about her limits, thoughts, and needs. She then began learning ways to communicate assertively in order to express her feelings, protect her time, and deal with various situations as they arose.

As Angie worked to feel valuable and good irrespective of her benevolent actions, her need to please others in an attempt to build self-esteem decreased. Eventually, Angie was able to communicate to Paul how much he'd hurt her feelings, discuss her workload with her boss, and politely turn down a request to help Alexandra with her next fund-raising event. To Angie's surprise, all three responded well and appreciated her honesty.

Do you relate to any aspect of Angie's story?

_____

_____

_____

_____

In what ways have you said yes when you wanted to say no to others?

_____

_____

_____

_____

What response might you expect if you were to take a step back and decline obligatory invitations or requests made by others? How would you feel?

_____

_____

_____

_____

 ## AVOIDING HIGH-RISK BEHAVIORS

Without assertiveness skills and healthy outlets, women with low self-esteem and issues of depression and anxiety sometimes turn to risky, self-destructive behaviors as a way to cope. Unhealthy coping strategies may include excessive drinking, drugs, promiscuity, or self-harmful behaviors. Initially, this can happen as a result of peer pressure or relinquishing your power in order to gain approval or feel wanted. While these activities may temporarily provide relief or distraction from the difficult emotions you are struggling with, they only serve as a Band-Aid over a greater problem that needs to be addressed.

Trying to build worth, gain approval, or decrease negative feelings by utilizing unhealthy coping mechanisms creates a vicious cycle, likely to leave you feeling even worse about yourself between fixes. Ultimately, these things are self-destructive and further damage self-esteem, in addition to creating serious and potentially dangerous health concerns and devastating problems with addiction.

If you are utilizing self-destructive behaviors as a way of coping, make a promise to yourself to stop in order to give yourself the time and space to work through the steps in this book. If you are unable to stop these behaviors on your own, seek out the help of a qualified professional who can support you through the process.

❑ Check this box if you need help breaking a destructive or dangerous habit, then write down the names and contact information for three potential providers who can help. (See Resources, page 201, for ways to find support.)

1. _____

2. _____

3. _____

Trusting Yourself

Part of respecting yourself involves developing self-trust. This can be a challenging task when self-esteem is low, especially after years of doubting your own worth, but like assertiveness, trust is something that can be cultivated and developed. Learning to trust your gut, your ability to make appropriate decisions, and the validity of your feelings are important pursuits as you develop faith in yourself and make changes to support a healthier future. Self-trust is an important component to following through with the steps in this program.

Circle true or false in response to the following statements:

I trust myself to . . .

1. Make good decisions   TRUE   FALSE

2. Care for my own well-being   TRUE   FALSE

3. Engage in healthy relationships   TRUE   FALSE

4. Walk away from harmful relationships   TRUE   FALSE

5. Put the tools I am learning into practice   TRUE   FALSE

6. Stay motivated to build self-esteem   TRUE   FALSE

If you answered "false" to any of these questions, consider finding a qualified therapist who can help you work through the steps on this journey. Sometimes, having an objective and supportive third party to hold you accountable can help you work through the issues that threaten your progress.

In *The Courage to Trust: A Guide to Building Deep and Loving Relationships*, Cynthia Wall describes three ways to begin the process of learning to trust yourself, including 1) Speaking kindly to yourself, 2) Avoiding people who undermine your self-trust, and 3) Keeping promises to yourself. These three things align perfectly with the steps and goals we are discussing regarding building self-esteem.

As you continue banishing the negative, distorted self-talk filled with preoccupation about what others think, replace these thoughts with self-talk that nurtures your gut instincts and abilities. Pay attention to how you act and react in various experiences, and focus on the emotions and physical sensations in your body. They can serve as a guide to tuning in to your own thoughts, beliefs, and personal requirements. Trust yourself to appropriately handle or walk away from uncomfortable situations.

As you work to develop self-respect and end the drive to people-please, work to avoid people who make this endeavor difficult for you. You may not have been able to avoid these people in the past, but as you increase your awareness, you can choose to take control and make choices about your relationships. We will talk more in the next step about ways to maintain healthy boundaries and supportive relationships.

You have already made the commitment to read this book and have made it this far—this is great news! Keep the momentum going by promising yourself to follow through with your journey to improve self-esteem! Meanwhile, continue practicing and ensuring you are utilizing the tools you've learned so far as you prepare to move on to the final two steps.

Look Back to Move Forward

In this chapter, you learned that developing a kind, affirmative internal voice filled with positive messages is at the forefront of every attempt to better care for and respect yourself. Continue to think about ways that you can practice demonstrating self-respect.

As you move forward:

Take stock of values. Assess the values that are most important to you. Ensure that these values are upheld in your life by how you treat and talk to yourself, and that they are reflected in what you expect and allow from others.

Don't over-sacrifice. Watch out for the tendency to sacrifice your own needs or well-being as you give in to others. Doing so reinforces messages and feelings that cause low self-esteem to endure. Beware of people-pleasing and the desire to gain approval and acceptance, as self-esteem cannot be built through external validation.

Replace negative self-talk. Pay attention to any distorted thinking and negative self-talk that prevents you from acting in ways that demonstrate self-respect. Replace negative self-talk with positive thoughts and affirmations.

Practice assertiveness skills. This will help you to act with confidence and self-respect during moments of decision or conflict. As you learn to trust yourself, allow your instincts to guide you.

Choose healthy spaces. Make an effort to avoid people and situations that make it difficult for you to feel good or act in self-respecting ways.

Make time for self-care. Continue to practice affirmations, healthy self-talk, and being kind to yourself. Add to your list of affirmations new statements that focus on self-respect and assertiveness.

Keep your promises. As you continue working toward improved self-esteem, stay true to your promise to make positive changes and implement the recommendations you learn in these steps.

Write about what you have learned in this chapter and how you can continue moving forward toward improving self-esteem.

_____

_____

_____

_____

Think about your own level of self-respect and your ability to trust your gut. Write about what you feel, and consider how you can use these feelings to stay strong on the path toward building self-esteem.

_____

_____

_____

_____

TAKE ACTION!

1. Choose one value that is important to you and focus on ways you can uphold that value in every interaction you encounter this week.
2. Write your name in your calendar or day planner as you schedule time for you!
3. Turn down one obligatory request or invitation in the next few weeks and write about how that makes you feel.
4. Practice expressing an opinion or making a request in a low-conflict situation.
5. Pay attention to the feelings, emotions, and sensations you experience in your body in various situations. Write down or think about what you felt.

• • • • •

Accept Yourself

ONCE YOU HAVE MADE STRIDES in getting to know yourself and have committed to practicing better self-care and treating yourself with respect, the next step is to develop true acceptance of who you are. This is a real turning point in the path to self-esteem. Accepting yourself involves coming to terms with the reality of your humanity, accepting your limits, acknowledging your shortcomings, and recognizing that maintaining healthy self-esteem is a lifelong journey.

In previous chapters we've discussed how gaining perspective and realistic standards are key to finding the self-acceptance necessary to build self-esteem. This step is where you really begin to recognize and accept yourself as imperfect yet whole. Until you truly accept yourself, you will remain vulnerable to the devastating effects of negative self-talk and distorted messages that block the path toward improved self-esteem.

Write about where you currently stand with self-acceptance. Does that term bring you discomfort, or are you able to think about it with a sense of purpose?

_____

_____

_____

_____

Do you recognize any strides you have made in terms of accepting yourself?

_____

_____

_____

_____

Self-acceptance doesn't happen in a moment; rather, it is an evolution. It involves working through your feelings and dissecting your past experiences to come to appreciate who you are. It's about acknowledging the different traits, experiences, and encounters that make up your existence, and coming to terms with the fact that you are going to have weaknesses. Self-acceptance is about being okay with yourself no matter what has happened or where you are today. In this chapter, you'll learn how to ward off the demons that can sabotage self-esteem as you develop a more secure and forgiving view of yourself.

Acknowledging Limits and Imperfections

One of the biggest challenges to accepting ourselves is recognizing and admitting that we have limits, flaws, and weaknesses. These things are all part of the human experience, yet they can be difficult to accept! Part of building self-esteem involves coming to terms with what these imperfections are and accepting them, rather than belittling ourselves for our failure to be perfect.

Eliminating perfectionism is vital to finding self-acceptance. As you move forward, pay attention to the unrealistic goals and expectations you continue to set for yourself—watch out for those times you are pulled toward the unrealistic standards in our society. Also, notice times when you fall into patterns of putting others first, giving away your power, or denying yourself the care and attention you inherently deserve.

Write about any struggles you continue to encounter, in terms of unrealistic goals, demanding expectations, or difficulty prioritizing your own needs:

_____

_____

_____

_____

Often, we make things more difficult for ourselves by denying, repressing, resisting, or fighting against imperfections or things we deem as flaws. But learning to find acceptance for every aspect of yourself—flaws included—empowers you and allows you to move forward. For example, if you beat yourself up over perfectionist tendencies, you are probably somebody who is really committed to detail. If you hate your wrinkles, try to see them as laugh lines showing years of a full life. No matter what your flaws, the first step toward acceptance is acknowledgment. When you are having a hard time or facing a difficult emotion, stop and acknowledge it. Sometimes acknowledging is all that is needed to move you from resistance to acceptance.

List three areas where you could develop greater acceptance:

1. _____
2. _____
3. _____

Can you identify any things that have prevented you from being accepting regarding the items you listed?

_____

_____

_____

_____

Resistance or failure to acknowledge imperfections often stems from fear—fear of being judged by others or of having feelings of worthlessness confirmed. Acknowledging weaknesses and accepting that human shortcomings do not diminish our value is vital in the process of building self-esteem.

Complete the following sentences and see if you can identify any negative self-talk or distorted thinking in your responses.

What Imperfection Means to Me

If I'm not perfect, _____

If I acknowledge my flaws, _____

If others see my weaknesses, _____

Hiding my weaknesses will _____

Being perfect means _____

What irrational beliefs, distorted self-talk, or negative messages exist in your answers?

_____

_____

_____

_____

Reframe them here:

_____

_____

_____

_____

Dealing with Criticism

We've already discussed what to do with negative self-talk and the importance of reframing messages from your inner critic. But how should you handle criticism from others? Dealing with criticism involves another layer of acceptance—acceptance not only that you are imperfect and therefore subject to criticism, but also that the world is a critical place, full of judgment, opinions, and unsolicited feedback.

When self-esteem is low, it's easy to take criticism personally and allow it to further deplete feelings of self-worth. The trouble is, there will always be criticism, but criticism is not necessarily a bad thing. There are two kinds of criticism: criticism that is constructive and meant to help move you forward toward growth and development, and criticism that is destructive and meant to cause you humiliation and discomfort.

Can you think of two examples, either experienced or made up, of each kind of criticism?

Constructive Criticism:

1. _____

2. _____

Destructive Criticism:

1. _____

2. _____

Write about how you tend to react to each kind of criticism, using either general thoughts of how you might react or specific reactions to real times you've encountered criticism in the past.

I tend to react to constructive criticism by:

_____

_____

_____

_____

I tend to react to destructive criticism by:

_____

_____

_____

_____

If your self-esteem is low, chances are you react either passively or aggressively to any form of criticism. The problem lies in automatically believing the validity of the criticism, allowing it to serve as "proof" that you are damaged and unworthy. It's not the criticism that hurts your self-esteem; rather, it's how you *think* about the criticism that does the damage.

Think of a specific time you received criticism. Can you identify what thoughts were going through your mind in response to the criticism?

_____

_____

_____

_____

As you work toward accepting yourself, your weaknesses, and your limits, take a close look at your reactions to criticism. When you react to criticism with aggression, such as acting defensively or counterattacking, this can lead to conflict in relationships and feelings of guilt and remorse that threaten self-esteem. When you react with passivity, you put the person delivering the criticism in a position of power, automatically believing their viewpoint and assuming the criticism is valid. You may shut down and surrender to the critic, either apologizing or remaining silent. In doing so, you fail to protect yourself, further reinforcing low self-esteem, and setting the tone to yourself and others that you are open to being taken advantage of.

Sometimes women react by using a combination of passive and aggressive behaviors. You may act passively in the moment but allow resentment and anger to build up to the point that you lash out in retaliation at the criticizer later, in some other aggressive way.

Do you identify with any of these behaviors? If so, in what way?

_____

_____

_____

The best way to handle criticism is to learn to accept constructive criticism and to respond to destructive criticism in an assertive manner. Stop and consider whether the criticism is actually valid and accurate, rather than just accepting it without deliberation. Whether or not criticism is warranted, you can protect your self-esteem by stopping to take a closer look at the critical message. In doing so, you internalize the message that your point of view matters. Your feelings, opinions, and thoughts are just as important as those of the critic. If a criticism is meant to be constructive and helpful, it's fine to thank the critic for the feedback and move on. If the criticism does not seem valid or warranted, respond in a rational, calm manner, using assertiveness skills to defend your position.

You can prepare yourself to handle criticism of any sort with confidence. Select one of the following affirmations and commit to keeping it in mind when you are responding to criticism:

- ☐ There are lots of opinions and viewpoints in the world.
- ☐ My thoughts are as important as those of anyone else.
- ☐ I handle conflict with ease.
- ☐ I am a calm and rational person.
- ☐ I am able to accept feedback from others.
- ☐ I see the bigger picture.

How you react and what you say are important things to consider because your reactions demonstrate and reinforce your level of self-esteem. Most important, however, is how you _think_ internally about critical messages.

If you are dealing with somebody who is abusive, narcissistic, or incapable of handling your assertiveness in an equally calm and respectful manner, it may not be useful or even safe for you to defend yourself against the criticism. In these cases, rather than speak up, you may need to let the criticism go, but use your internal dialogue to remind yourself that you are not the problem.

RESPONDING TO CRITICISM

The following scenarios provide examples of three different ways to respond to criticism. Choose the option that seems like the best response for each situation.

1. Your partner tells you he/she doesn't like the paint color you've chosen for the living room. You reply:
   a. "What are you talking about? You don't know anything about decorating!"
   b. "Well, pick whatever you want then."
   c. "Really? I think it's a great color. Tell me what you don't like about it."

2. You arrive 15 minutes late to meet your friend for dinner. Frustrated, she exclaims, "You're always late!" You respond:
   a. "I'm sorry," and feel terrible about yourself for making her annoyed.
   b. "I am late. The traffic was horrible!"
   c. "Well you're the one who picked a restaurant on the other side of town!"

3. You get an e-mail from your boss, saying, "The file I reviewed had a lot of mistakes that should have been corrected." You respond by:
   a. Firing off a response that says, "If I had gotten a little more notice on this project I could have spent more time fixing all the errors other people made."
   b. Ignoring the e-mail and spending the rest of the day feeling terrible, thinking about how your boss hates you and you aren't very good at your job.
   c. E-mailing back, saying, "Thanks for your feedback. Do you have time today to meet to discuss ways it can be improved?"

4. Your mother criticizes your children's outfits, saying, "Is that really what they are wearing to the party? They look like they just rolled out of bed!" You:
   a. Exclaim, "I think they look adorable in whatever they have on! Let's go, everyone!"
   b. Ignore her as you walk past and help the kids put on their coats.
   c. Snap at her in an exasperated tone, saying, "Maybe if you would have gotten off the couch and helped me this morning, I would have had time to iron their shirts."

5. Your partner has demonstrated a tendency to lose his/her cool and become insulting and degrading when angry. Although physical violence has never occurred, you do wonder if things could escalate to that point. Today, you come home in a good mood after dinner with your friends and your partner accuses you of cheating, screaming at you, calling you hurtful names, and making all kinds of false accusations. You respond by:

   a. Telling your partner, "You have no right to treat me this way. I am not going to let your unfounded jealousy ruin my night."
   b. Calling your partner crazy and yelling back about what a terrible person he/she is.
   c. Breaking down, crying, swearing you didn't do anything wrong, and begging your partner not to be mad at you.

In these various examples of criticism, the appropriate responses are: 1) C, 2) B, 3) C, 4) A, 5) A. However, a word of caution regarding example number 5: Because you are dealing with an irrational, potentially abusive person, you have to be very careful about your response. Acting *too* assertively in relationships where there is dysfunction or a potential for abuse can increase your risk of being hurt or emotionally abused.

The safest option in the short term might be to tone down your assertive message to something short and simple, like "I did not do anything wrong" and walk away from the situation, while thinking to yourself, "This person has some major insecurity issues that I do not need to let affect my sense of identity." The safest option in the long term may be to rethink that unhealthy relationship going forward. Remember, how you think internally is the most important part of protecting self-esteem. (Note: The more you develop assertiveness skills and learn to filter out harmful criticisms, the closer you will become to building the self-esteem necessary to get out of or mitigate the effects of unhealthy relationships that bring you down.)

Write about your biggest challenge in terms of reacting to criticism (either internally or externally), and name two ways you can work to improve your reaction to criticism:

_____

_____

_____

_____

_____

_____

_____

_____

Accepting Your Strengths and Weaknesses

Another important aspect to self-acceptance and building self-esteem is knowing your strengths and weaknesses and owning both sides. While strengths are easier to accept, women with low self-esteem often have a difficult time listing their strengths and find it much easier to pinpoint their weaknesses. Knowing yourself and building self-esteem involves recognizing both.

Think about your strengths, including traits you like, characteristics you are proud of, and skills and talents you possess. It's important to make an effort to regularly give yourself praise or a pat on the back for the things you do well. Remember that it takes several positives to outweigh a negative, so give yourself ample credit for all of your strengths, using affirmations to acknowledge them and celebrate yourself. In the space provided, list six of your strengths. Write affirmations that show appreciation for these things.

RECOGNIZING STRENGTHS

Examples

STRENGTH	AFFIRMATION
Hardworking	*I take pride in my dedication to working hard.*
Artistic	*I am artistically talented.*

STRENGTH	AFFIRMATION
1. _____	_____
2. _____	_____
3. _____	_____
4. _____	_____
5. _____	_____
6. _____	

In addition to recognizing strengths, it's important for you to come to terms with your weaknesses. Understand that building self-esteem is not about getting rid of weaknesses or seeking perfection, but rather, it's about accepting flaws and imperfections as a natural part of humanity. Weaknesses come in many forms, including skills we aren't adept at, personality flaws, and physical imperfections.

When you think about other people, it's probably easy to see that not everyone is going to be good at everything. We all have different levels of talent, knowledge, training, and understanding. Yet, despite this recognition, you may still hold yourself to different, higher standards than you do others. Remember the mention of Molly's "faulty ruler" in chapter 1 (page 4)? Reflect upon the ways you judge yourself more harshly than you do others.

_____

_____

_____

When self-esteem is low, we tend to have a difficult time accepting ourselves as human, fallible, and imperfect. We hold ourselves to the unrealistic expectations we've discussed throughout the book, setting us up to constantly feel inadequate and unworthy. To find self-acceptance, we must let go of these unrealistic measures and instead view ourselves from a realistic and compassionate frame of reference.

In the space provided, make a list of at least six of your weaknesses. Try to include a variety of types of weaknesses, such as things you perceive as physical flaws, personality faults, limits, disadvantages, and vulnerabilities. Next, create affirmations that speak to those weaknesses. Affirmations can reframe the weakness, demonstrate acceptance of it, or support movement toward healthier alternatives. See the following examples for inspiration.

REFRAMING WEAKNESSES

Examples

WEAKNESS	AFFIRMATION
Impatience	I am learning to slow down.
Forgetful	I have a lot on my plate.
Don't know how to set limits	I am learning to be assertive.
Hate being alone	I can spend time with myself.
Fat belly	My body grew two children.
Wrinkles on face	I am aging with grace.

WEAKNESS	AFFIRMATION
1.	
2.	
3.	
4.	
5.	
6.	

Accepting Your Mistakes

In the previous chapter, you identified values that you deem important (page 132). When self-esteem is low, it can be difficult to uphold these values. We've discussed how feelings of self-hatred or a desire to escape pain can lead you down a path of making poor decisions that go against your values. These decisions can lead to other bad decisions, like being dishonest and deceitful or engaging in self-destructive behaviors to hide or drown out mistakes. This creates a never-ending cycle of shame that blocks the possibility of building healthy self-esteem.

If you find yourself stuck in this type of pattern, take a step back and cut yourself some slack. In order to find self-acceptance, you will need to acknowledge your actions, accept the mistakes you've made as being just that—mistakes—and move on. Mistakes are an important part of our experience as humans—we all make them. Mistakes teach us valuable lessons and give us an opportunity to learn and grow. Once again, it's how you *think* about a mistake that dictates how you feel and ultimately determines whether the mistake will hold you back or move you forward.

Identify a mistake you recently made, and write about how you felt and what you told yourself in response to the mistake:

_____

_____

_____

_____

Can you identify any negative self-talk, irrational beliefs, or harmful messages in your thoughts? If so, write what they are. Explain why they are harmful.

_____

_____

_____

_____

If you identified any negative self-talk, reframe it into something more productive:

_____

_____

_____

_____

An important part of self-acceptance involves identifying the negative self-talk that results from any mistake or regret, and working to reframe negative messages into kinder, gentler language. Remember to talk to yourself like you would talk to a friend. If you look at each event through a broader, less critical lens, can you see the bigger picture? Can you identify any lessons that can come of this, or at least reframe the situation and decrease negative feelings as a result? When you focus on failures as opportunities for growth and learning, rather than reasons to condemn yourself, you greatly increase your chances of improving self-esteem.

Write down one way mistakes can be helpful:

_____

_____

_____

_____

Knowing Your Threshold for Stress

We all have a certain threshold for stress. When we exceed our capacity to effectively manage stress, we succumb to things like irritability, frustration, anger, fatigue, and desperation in our attempt to cope. Minor issues that would ordinarily be easily managed can put us over the edge when they all pile up at once.

Sometimes, dealing with more major stressors can lead to unhealthy coping strategies and defense mechanisms. Behaviors that may have helped you in the past can become habits and default ways of responding that can get in the way and pose challenges in the present. For example, avoidance may be a current obstacle to Jane's self-esteem; however, it may have been the only way she knew how to survive a dysfunctional childhood. Shutting down and dissociating may have been the way Jane survived abuse in the past, but it prevents her from having healthy and successful relationships in the present.

In instances where you find your own old coping habits persisting, strive to have compassion for yourself and recognize that growth and change require awareness, acceptance, and willingness to learn new ways of coping. Just like anyone else, you are vulnerable to stress getting the best of you. Recognize those times you are overwhelmed, and remember to treat yourself with kindness and ask for help when needed. It's healthy to acknowledge when you are having a hard time. Often this acknowledgment alone helps ease some of the discomfort. Part of learning to accept yourself involves recognizing what takes a toll on you emotionally and understanding that you sometimes need empathy and support.

List some signs that indicate you are nearing your threshold for stress:

_____

_____

_____

_____

List three ways you can alleviate some of your stress:

1. _____
2. _____
3. _____

List three people you can turn to for help and support:

1. _____
2. _____
3. _____

List three places you can go to find a sense of calm:

1. _____
2. _____
3. _____

SADIE'S STORY

Sadie was a client who had a history of childhood sexual abuse. She confessed that she was regularly abused by a family friend for several years and described how his threats and manipulation, along with her feelings of shame, prevented her from ever telling her parents.

Fighting off her abuser had led to threats of harm to her and her loved ones, so Sadie learned to submit. Shutting down and dissociating during the abuse was the only way she knew how to cope.

As an adult, Sadie carried with her the fear of being hurt and the habit of shutting down when she felt anxious in relationships. Anytime someone tried to get close to her, Sadie pushed them away, closing herself off emotionally. When she faced any form of discomfort, stress, or conflict in relationships, she ran away, avoiding the person without explanation. These behaviors left her feeling isolated, lonely, and broken. She told herself she was damaged and incapable of finding love.

Sadie also developed a habit of overeating to deal with her emotional pain. Anytime she experienced residual effects of trauma, felt lonely, or faced stress, she started snacking on junk food to fill the void. On one level, Sadie was disgusted with herself for her unhealthy eating habits; on another, she was happy about the fact that she was gaining weight, believing that being overweight might protect her from ever being assaulted again.

In therapy, Sadie began exploring the ways she was sabotaging relationships and preventing herself from having the happy, healthy life she deserved. She began opening up about the abuse, recognizing how her present struggles related to her past trauma. Sadie eventually was able to accept what had happened and recognize it was not her fault. She decided to forgive herself for the various ways she'd let the legacy of her abuse control her decisions and actions. She learned that she was okay and could develop healthy self-esteem despite what she went through. She began implementing new, healthy coping mechanisms and found that utilizing them during moments of stress helped her move forward with a greater sense of empowerment.

Do you relate to any aspects of Sadie's story?

_____

_____

_____

_____

Which of your past experiences have contributed to present-day behaviors you wish you could change?

_____

_____

_____

_____

What coping habits or patterns have you found yourself utilizing?

_____

_____

_____

_____

What results do you think you will experience when you begin utilizing healthy coping skills to manage your stress?

_____

_____

_____

_____

Forgiving Yourself and Others

Part of acceptance may involve a need to forgive, especially when it comes to your own shortcomings, mistakes, or personal challenges. Holding grudges and staying stuck in a place of regret, blame, and shame make it difficult to build self-esteem. While acceptance is about coming to terms with a circumstance or event, forgiveness is about processing and ultimately letting go of the feelings of guilt, hurt, anger, and resentment. In past chapters, we've looked at the ways our history, upbringing, and interactions guide our self-esteem. Part of moving forward toward self-esteem involves letting go of the past and finding forgiveness.

Forgiveness can be a tricky thing. Let me be clear that I do not mean you need to excuse or reconcile with people who have deeply hurt you. Doing so could demonstrate a devaluing of yourself that can inhibit self-esteem even further. Instead, I am talking about accepting that you cannot change others or the events of your past. You can, however, make choices in how you move forward. Choosing to let go of the past, accept what happened, and forgive (especially yourself) allows you to relinquish the hold the past has on your life and frees you up to focus on the future.

Write about any experiences you have had with forgiveness, of yourself or others:

_____

_____

_____

_____

Forgiveness is not about excusing poor behavior or forgetting something happened, nor is it about minimizing your feelings. It's simply about admitting and accepting things that have happened in order to move through the feelings and prevent them from keeping you trapped in a place of anger, regret, hurt, or shame. Forgiveness is something you do for yourself, not for anyone else. It brings you peace and allows you to move from being a victim to becoming a survivor, capable of moving on.

Steps to forgiveness involve:

- Acknowledging and accepting the reality of what happened
- Allowing yourself to experience and process your negative feelings
- Letting go and moving beyond the negative feelings

Forgiveness is a means of regaining control and taking back your power to find healing. Like much of what we've encountered in this book, forgiveness is a skill that can be learned and practiced. Simply being willing to consider forgiveness opens you up to the mind-set that brings about change and the possibility of self-acceptance and self-love. But first, let's figure out what needs forgiving.

List some people or situations that require your forgiveness in order for you to be free of past burdens and to move forward toward self-esteem with peace:

_____

_____

_____

It can be very helpful to tell your story to somebody you can trust. Research shows that sharing reduces shame, eliminates isolation, and brings about healing. If you don't have a supportive person you can confide in, seek out the help of a therapist or support group that can give you a safe place to open up about your experiences (see Resources, page 201) for help finding providers in your area).

When you identify someone you need to forgive or a situation you need to move beyond, consider writing a letter to that person, telling them how you feel and expressing your desire to accept what happened, rise above it, and let go of the contempt and hurt that hold you back. First, let me say that you don't need to give your letter to the person. Writing a letter of forgiveness or intent to move beyond an experience is an exercise just for you to help you process your feelings, and it can be a particularly powerful one. If you are inclined, you might consider editing your letter into a version you *can* share with the person, but doing so is not the goal of the exercise. Rather, the goal is to give yourself a space to express your hurt and process your feelings in order to release the hold these feelings have over you. Freeing yourself of wounds from the past can unlock the door to self-acceptance and, consequently, improved self-esteem.

LETTERS OF FORGIVENESS

Think about who or what in your life needs your forgiveness and acceptance in order for you to let go of the past and move toward a future filled with healthy self-esteem. Maybe it's someone else you need to forgive, or maybe it's yourself. In the space provided, write a letter to the person you most need to forgive. Write stream-of-consciousness style, letting whatever comes up flow onto the paper. Don't worry about spelling, punctuation, grammar, or even making sense. Remember, this experience is just for you, to help you release the past and move forward toward greater well-being. Once you are finished with the letter, decide what you want to do with it. Feel free to rip out the page and shred or burn it.

FINDING MEANING

As you work on forgiveness, look back on your responses to the exercises in previous chapters, including responses to the Low Self-Esteem checklist (page 15), the Initial Reflections (page 21), and the Rewriting Your Story exercise (page 99). Are there people in your life who you need to forgive, or experiences you need to accept, for you to move forward toward self-esteem with peace? With greater insight and self-awareness regarding how your current level of self-esteem may relate to prior experiences, can you find any meaning or useful lessons that stemmed from the struggles you've endured? Consider "Morgan's Story" (page 97), in which she concluded, "I had an experience that taught me that I can overcome and rise above anything that comes my way."

Psychologist and Holocaust survivor Viktor Frankl, in his book *Man's Search for Meaning*, described how striving for meaning is a primary motivational force for humans. He explained that it's the attitude we take toward situations that matters. Nobody can take away the attitude you choose to take in regard to any situation. Much like the fact that building self-esteem involves making the choice to use positive self-talk, gaining self-acceptance involves making the choice to have a positive attitude aimed at learning and growth. When we can find meaning in our struggles, we can transform personal challenges and trage-dies into triumphs and successes.

Lessons Learned

In the space provided, reflect upon any lessons you've learned as a result of your struggles. With the self-compassion you are working to develop, are you able to cut yourself some slack and find a greater level of self-acceptance regarding how you handled various situations in your past?

_____

_____

_____

_____

_____

COPING WITH SETBACKS

No one has a constant level of healthy self-esteem. Life's challenges can test even the strongest self-esteem. As you work through the steps in this book, you may stay very motivated to move forward toward positive growth, and that's awesome. Working with self-esteem tools can be relatively straightforward when life is going smoothly. But inevitably, life will throw you a curveball that interferes with your remembering to put your skills and tools into action.

Building and maintaining self-esteem is a lifelong process that involves continuous use of the skills and action items presented in this book. Stressors, setbacks, tragedies, and the chaos of life all have the potential to derail your progress, but it is during these very times that it's especially necessary to utilize these skills to protect your self-esteem and maintain your hard-earned sense of well-being.

Recognize that there will be bumps along the way that will threaten the progress you've made and lead to a relapse in negative self-talk and other symptoms of low self-esteem. Building and maintaining self-esteem often means two steps forward and one step back. Please don't get caught up in anger and frustration at the arrows life throws your way. Rather, pay attention to the attitude you take during these moments of challenge and draw from this; recognize that you are gaining strength and learning invaluable lessons along the way.

Look Back to Move Forward

Before moving forward to the final step in your journey, let's review some of the main points of this chapter. An important step in building self-esteem involves coming to terms with yourself, your past, and the experiences that have brought you to where you are today. Learning to embrace and accept all aspects of yourself is vital to the process.

As you move forward, continue to:

Recognize your strengths. Continuously use affirmations to give yourself praise.

Own your flaws. Accept your limitations and imperfections, recognizing that weaknesses are part of being human. Use affirmations to develop self-acceptance and counter the effects of ruminating over flaws and imper-fections. Think about what it means to be perfect and how lowering your personal standards and expectations will help you find increased peace and harmony.

Handle criticism effectively. Work to respond to criticism in effective, self-protecting ways. Be wary of abusive people or situations that interfere with your progress and continue to practice the skills you are learning in safe environments.

Forgive yourself. Accept your mistakes and missteps, recognizing that there are reasons and roots behind your actions. Acknowledging these things and letting go of guilt and regrets can open you up to moving forward with courage and compassion.

Forgive others. Remember that forgiveness is about letting go and moving on rather than condoning, excusing, or forgetting. Know that you have to feel to heal, and that activities like sharing and expressing can help move you through this process.

Stay mindful. Watch out for setbacks that may derail your progress or dis-tract you from your mission to build healthy self-esteem, and work to transform setbacks into triumphs with an attitude of hope and positivity.

Write about your biggest takeaway from this chapter and how you can use it to continue improving your self-esteem.

_____

_____

_____

_____

Think about where you stand with regard to self-acceptance. Write about what you feel, and consider how you can use these feelings to continue building self-esteem.

_____

_____

_____

_____

_____

_____

_____

_____

_____

TAKE ACTION!

1. Create affirmations praising your strengths and accepting your flaws. Write them on sticky notes, and strategically place them where you will see them daily.
2. The next time you near your stress threshold this week, ask someone for help.
3. Write one mistake that happened this week, and decide how you can use it as an opportunity to learn or grow.
4. Pay attention to your initial reaction to a criticism this week, and see if you can respond with confidence.
5. Search "forgiveness quotes" on Google and choose three that inspire you. Write down your favorites and read them daily.

Love Yourself

ACCEPTING YOURSELF SETS THE STAGE for loving yourself, which is the final step in your journey to obtaining healthy self-esteem. When you are truly able to love yourself, you become capable of treating yourself with the compassion, flexibility, and affection that are so important to maintaining self-esteem throughout life. Loving yourself involves acknowledging and accepting that you *deserve* love and that others around you benefit from your love; not only your love for them, but for yourself as well.

There's a reason that many of the buzzwords and steps in this journey involve the word *self*—self-esteem, self-worth, self-knowledge, self-care, self-respect, and self-acceptance. You cannot accomplish any of these things through external means. Building self-esteem and cultivating a life of confidence and inner strength requires you to turn inward, take small risks for positive change, and embrace vulnerability, all things that are most successfully accomplished when backed by love and support.

By accepting and loving yourself from within, you can maintain healthy, loving relationships built on mutual respect. Strong relationships require self-esteem, and they also help to support it. When we love ourselves and others, we can reap the important benefits of healthy self-esteem.

Pause for a moment and think about your relationship with yourself. How do you currently feel? Do you like yourself? Are you able to love yourself? Write your thoughts on this subject:

_____

_____

_____

_____

The idea of self-love may seem simplistic; however, it's often one of the most difficult steps to achieve for women with low self-esteem, who have likely suffered years of believing they are not lovable. Truly loving yourself can require hard work and a willingness to be vulnerable, but the rewards are immense. It may feel silly or foreign at first to think about loving yourself, but accessing the ability to cultivate self-love has an enormous impact on the path that awaits you beyond this journey. In this chapter, you will learn how to love and protect yourself in ways that will foster healthy self-esteem.

You Deserve Love

It's worth repeating that you possess inherent, unwavering worth as a human. You also have a basic, intrinsic need for love and belonging. We all do. Receiving love, comfort, and support is part of our birthright. Unfortunately, the sense of being unconditionally loved may not have happened for everyone from the start or somehow may have been lost along the way, but the best person to give you the love you need and deserve *now* is you.

You are the *only* person who will be there and available for you 100 percent of the time, 24/7, for the rest of your life. Nobody else truly knows the full extent of your history, struggles, tragedies, and triumphs the way you do, so it makes good sense that you strive to be your own best friend rather than your own worst critic.

Write down three ways you can treat yourself like a best friend:

1. _____

2. _____

3. _____

Loving yourself involves some key ideals, including:

· Believing in your worth
· Caring for yourself
· Caring about your future
· Comforting yourself when needed
· Being moved by your own pain and struggles
· Treating yourself with the same kindness, support, respect, and compassion that you would give to a dear friend or a loved one

Demonstrating self-love may be difficult, especially for women who grew up in families in which emotions were not expressed. The more you practice, the easier it will become. Give it a try, even with a "fake it until you make it" attitude.

Women's health expert Christiane Northrup recommends taking the 21-Day Self-Esteem Challenge, which entails standing in front of the mirror, staring at yourself, and saying, "I love you, I really love you" for 21 days in a row—21 days representing the length of time some researchers believe it takes to form a new habit via consistent practice. Try doing this exercise consistently for at least 21 days as you move forward with expressing self-love and pay attention to how it feels.

Write about how it feels the very first time:

_____

_____

_____

_____

How does it feel after a week of daily practice?

_____

_____

_____

_____

In previous chapters, we talked a lot about nurturing your mind through healthy self-talk and positive affirmations and caring for your physical and mental health through a dedication to self-care. Self-love goes beyond these things and is about truly nurturing your spirit and your soul. By becoming mindful of your need for self-love and dedicating your energy to loving yourself, you can lock in all of the gains and wisdom you've acquired along this journey toward building healthy self-esteem.

Self-love is accomplished by setting the intention to accept yourself while demonstrating unconditional positive regard for yourself despite anything that comes your way, including weaknesses, flaws, missteps, and imperfections. Consider the unconditional way you would love a child, a pet, or a soul mate and strive to turn that unwavering love inward. Remember that having healthy self-esteem and exhibiting self-love is not the same as being narcissistic or arrogant. These things only occur when you disrespect others and care for yourself at the expense of others' well-being.

Here are a few examples of the differences between healthy self-esteem and narcissism. Think about characteristics you've seen or could imagine seeing in others and add them to the list.

SELF-ESTEEM	NARCISSISM
Respectful of others	Controlling or demeaning others
Self-assured	Insecure
Self-confident	Fearful of judgment
Humble	Grandiose

Self-love is a gift you give, not only to yourself but also to the people and world around you. There is an endless supply of love, and when you love yourself, you are better able to love others and receive their love in return. One of my clients recently put this so eloquently, saying, "I realized that when people say, 'You need to love yourself before you can be loved,' they mean you just need to be able to *accept* someone loving you to be loved." Accepting love from others involves believing in your ability to be loved through loving yourself first.

Imagine yourself as a tree in nature. You require sunlight and water to survive, grow, and flourish. Using the illustration provided, plot out some of what you need to grow and thrive. Use the sun, its rays, and the cloud and raindrops to write in anything you can think of that you need to nourish your spirit and provide yourself with love and support. Then use the leaves of the tree to identify the ways your self-esteem will benefit from your love and self-nurturing. You may want to write down things we've already discussed and pinpointed in previous steps, and you can add anything new that comes to mind for what you personally need and plan to implement in order to practice self-love. Keep the image of your completed tree in mind as you put into practice the lessons you have learned along this journey.

SELF-LOVE TREE

Celebrating Yourself and Your Progress

Think about and appreciate how complex and miraculous life can be. The fact that a giant tree can sprout from tiny seeds, water, and sunlight is pretty amazing. Regardless of your spiritual, religious, or existential belief system, hopefully you can see that your existence, too, is remarkable. When you step back and recognize yourself as one unique individual, it may be easier to see yourself through a lens of admiration, in which you can truly celebrate your existence.

The visual of your self-love tree can help you recognize all the complicated pieces involved in sustaining your well-being and living a good life. Seeing just how much you need to give yourself in order to grow well and achieve self-esteem allows you to appreciate your efforts and recognize the importance of staying motivated to cultivate your best self. When you realize the bigger picture of all you are doing to support and enhance yourself, how can you not love someone so dedicated and wonderful?

Although past struggles may not bring about celebratory feelings, the fact that you are strong enough to devote the time and effort to reading this book and working through its steps shows that you recognize the importance of investing in yourself. That alone is something to be hopeful about.

Give yourself credit for any progress you have made so far, including the smallest of baby steps. Write down three praiseworthy things you have done so far on your journey to healthy self-esteem:

1. _____

2. _____

3. _____

Rather than be humble about your efforts, give yourself permission to applaud yourself for them. Even if you have not yet made great strides or mastered the tasks outlined in previous chapters, you are still developing a greater awareness of what it takes to move toward healthy self-esteem, and that is a big step in and of itself. By simply being open to learning ways to improve yourself, you are moving in the right direction.

Using the space provided, write a love letter to yourself, celebrating your knowledge, applauding yourself for your dedication, and professing your eternal commitment to yourself and a future filled with healthy self-esteem. It may feel awkward to write a love letter to yourself, but who's to judge? Ignore any feelings of reluctance, modesty, or discomfort around this exercise, and just write from your heart. Allowing yourself to open up to heartfelt expression will unlock the door to self-love.

LOVE LETTER TO MYSELF

Accepting Compliments

You may have found it difficult to give yourself loving feedback, and that's okay. If you were unable to write yourself a letter, consider coming back to this exercise later, after you've read through more of the chapter and gained some experience practicing self-love. If you found writing a love letter to yourself to be challenging, write about what feelings emerged and what got in your way:

_____

_____

_____

_____

Building self-esteem involves learning to be comfortable with receiving compliments—this includes those from yourself as well as from others. Accepting compliments can be particularly difficult for women with low self-esteem who do not feel worthy of love and praise. While you may crave compliments and validation, as we have learned, you cannot build self-esteem externally. When self-esteem is low, you are likely to react to compliments with negative self-talk and responses that minimize, deny, or discredit the compliment completely.

When you receive compliments, pay attention to your initial reactions. Do you tend to dismiss or diminish the praise that comes your way? Write about what happens for you:

_____

_____

_____

_____

Now imagine yourself giving a compliment to someone—a friend, a family member, or a coworker. Imagine what words you might say, then envision how they might react. What would it feel like to be met with resistance or denial?

Practice giving compliments to others this week. Keep track of five compliments you give and the responses you receive. What do you notice about how people respond to compliments?

WHO	COMPLIMENT	RESPONSE
Coworker	*"I love your haircut!"*	*"Oh, it's way too short."*
Friend	*"You look great! I love that shirt!"*	*"I'm trying to hide the weight gain."*

1. _____
   _____
2. _____
   _____
3. _____
   _____
4. _____
   _____
5. _____
   _____

When we consider it from the angle of the other person, it's pretty clear that it's nicer when the person accepts our compliment with a smile and a thank-you. Rejecting compliments not only reinforces low self-esteem but also discredits the person delivering the compliment.

ACKNOWLEDGING COMPLIMENTS

With an understanding that blocking compliments hampers self-love, pay close attention to any compliments you receive during the next week. You can respect yourself and the opinions and words of others by breaking the habit of deflecting compliments. Instead, work to accept them with grace, allowing them to sink in, and respond with a simple thank-you. On the following page, write down any compliments you receive, and note whether you felt the urge to discredit them. Write about whether you were able to respond with acceptance. If not, what thoughts or feelings got in the way?

COMPLIMENT	MY RESPONSE	HOW I FELT

How Self-Esteem Impacts Relationships

The relationship you have with yourself sets the stage and lays the groundwork for every other relationship in your life. Self-esteem allows us to have healthy relationships with partners, family, friends, and other significant people in our lives. Our self-esteem is not an unmoving entity that exists in a vacuum—rather, it intersects with other people and their respective levels of self-esteem, too. The repercussions of relationships that involve low self-esteem within one or both people can be astounding.

Research shows that people who are highly self-critical tend to be dissatisfied in their relationships. They judge themselves and assume others judge them just as harshly, thus displaying oversensitivity and defensiveness in their interactions. This undermines closeness in relationships, preventing trust, intimacy, and effective communication, instead creating distance, loneliness, and a lack of support that pose a threat to self-love.

What have you experienced regarding self-esteem and your relationships with others?

_____

_____

_____

_____

With low self-esteem, you may inadvertently act in ways that negatively impact healthy and otherwise stable relationships, creating a vicious cycle where low self-esteem and relationship dysfunction reinforce one another. Some consequences of low self-esteem in a relationship involve constantly feeling like a victim, being passive or aggressive, acting in needy or clingy ways, or testing (and ultimately sabotaging) positive relationships. Any of these behaviors have the potential to ruin relationships, leaving you feeling isolated and alone.

Low self-esteem also increases your susceptibility to forming unhealthy relationships. Without healthy self-esteem, you may rely too much on others, allowing them to assume all of the power. This increases your vulnerability of being taken advantage of, succumbing to peer pressure, or finding yourself stuck in relationships that involve patterns of abuse.

Can you think of any situations or relationships that were unhealthy for you? How might things have been different if, at the time, you loved and respected yourself more?

_____

_____

_____

_____

As you think about your self-esteem and your interactions with the people in your life, reflect upon whether you engage in behaviors that prevent you from having healthy relationships. It may help to look back over your responses to the Low Self-Esteem checklist (page 15). Did you check anything that might contribute to problematic exchanges in your relationships? If so, consider what it would take to make changes to decrease or end these behaviors. Think about how loving yourself will change your relationships for the better. In the space provided, write about the differences and benefits the people in your life will experience as a result of your learning to love yourself.

HOW LOVING YOURSELF WILL AFFECT YOUR LOVE FOR OTHERS

_____

_____

_____

_____

_____

_____

_____

_____

_____

Creating Boundaries

Loving yourself involves distancing yourself from the people in your life who do not respect your welfare and therefore do not deserve your love and attention. People who are unable to show you love, or who treat you in unloving ways, are toxic to your growth, well-being, and efforts to build self-esteem. When we love ourselves and have healthy self-esteem, we are less likely to tolerate abusive or unhealthy relationships. Discovering self-love makes it easier to walk away from unhealthy situations and rid ourselves of the toxic people that bring us down.

You may have people in your life who you cannot escape or completely separate yourself from—perhaps a toxic parent, an abusive family member, an ex with whom you co-parent, or a negative coworker. When this is the case, your best course of action is to work to establish better boundaries that allow you to protect and respect yourself. Boundaries are the limits and rules we set in relationships that guide others to know what we will and will not tolerate. Loving yourself demonstrates a precedent that others will follow.

ANYA'S STORY

Anya came to therapy at the insistence of her parents, who were frustrated that she was "failing to launch." Anya was in her late twenties but still lived with her parents, whom she relied on for financial support. She had dropped out of college during her junior year and gone from one temp job to the next, feeling dissatisfied with the work and discouraged about where her future would take her.

As I got to know Anya, I began to sense that her home life was rather chaotic, with a lot of fighting, name-calling, and criticism. Her decision to drop out of college was mostly due to her parents' lack of support and enthusiasm for the degree in education that she wanted to pursue. They had a different vision for her future and let it be known that her choices led to perpetual disappointments. She admitted feeling like she could never do anything right by her parents and said dropping out of college was a result of feeling there was no point in pushing herself when she'd just be met with judgment.

Without a steady job, Anya was unable to move out of her parents' house, but staying there was toxic to her well-being. She reported that fights often escalated to the point of violent outbursts, with dishes being broken and her running out of the house and sleeping at a friend's.

Anya's work in therapy involved recognizing that she had the right to make her own decisions and feel confident in them. She also strived to gain a better understanding regarding where her parents might be coming from. While they might not be "right," they were entitled to their feelings, and she realized that while she could not change them, she could change the way she interacted with them.

Anya practiced assertiveness skills and worked to find a balance between respecting her parents while also acting in her own best interest. As she gained confidence and grew stronger, Anya became firmer with her parents, telling them she would not tolerate violence or name-calling, and that she was only willing to talk to them when everyone remained calm. When conversations did become heated, rather than storming out, Anya politely said, "I need to take a break." She'd then write her thoughts to her parents in an e-mail, a solution that gave her the space to process her thoughts without their interruptions or accusations.

At first, Anya's parents felt that her boundary-setting and ultimatums were a threat to their authority, but they eventually realized that playing by the rules she was enforcing led to more peace in their relationship. Feeling proud of herself for leading the way toward a more mutually respectful relationship, Anya's self-esteem continued to grow. Eventually, she was able to tell her parents she planned to return to school to pursue her dream career as a teacher and that she hoped they would respect her decision, even though it wasn't their first choice.

Have you ever been in a situation like Anya's? If so, describe how you handled it. Were you able to establish boundaries? Whether you were able to or not, what were the results?

_____

_____

_____

_____

What would it take for you to consistently demonstrate assertiveness and boundary-setting?

_____

_____

_____

_____

Can you identify three situations in your life in which setting boundaries will help protect your self-esteem?

1. _____
2. _____
3. _____

As you begin exercising self-love and self-respect, the people in your life will need to shift to accommodate and align with these changes. For some, this may be a challenge. Any change, even those for the better, can be difficult. You may be met with resistance as others demonstrate reluctance in adapting to your new ways of interacting that accompany your improving level of self-esteem. Don't let this discourage you. The more you persist with setting boundaries through the use of assertiveness skills, the easier it will become. The dual payoff of enhanced self-esteem and healthier relationships will make this well worth the effort.

As you move forward with new relationships, make healthy choices about the people you surround yourself with. Choose people who help support your vision of who you want to be and who empower your self-esteem. Find positive mentors, role models, and friends to make up your emotional support network. Look back at your support network in the exercise you completed in step 2 (page 125). If you do not already have positive, healthy connections in your micro network, work to establish relationships that meet these criteria.

 ## VOLUNTEERING FOR YOURSELF

Research has shown that volunteering leads to physical and mental health benefits, including improved self-esteem, especially when the volunteer work involves helping strangers. Volunteering provides a sense of purpose, chances to interact with others, feelings of belonging, and opportunities to learn new skills, gain new experiences, and develop a sense of achievement. When you choose to volunteer, you demonstrate the conviction that you have something worth offering to others, which in and of itself reinforces your self-esteem.

There are countless ways to volunteer and make a difference in the world and in your own life. Look for opportunities in your community at animal shelters, nursing homes, hospitals, homeless or domestic violence shelters, food banks, churches, and local cleanup efforts. In the space provided, list at least five potential volunteer opportunities with phone numbers or websites. Doing so can help contribute to your efforts to build healthy self-esteem.

VOLUNTEER OPPORTUNITY   CONTACT INFO

_____   _____

_____   _____

_____   _____

_____   _____

_____   _____

Compassion for Yourself and Others

Give yourself a hug! When you treat yourself with compassion and kindness, you are more capable of ensuring that you surround yourself with healthy, loving, and supportive relationships, while minimizing your time with people who contaminate your sense of well-being. Simply put, if you look out for yourself like you would a good friend, you're less likely to tolerate people who make you feel negatively. Loving and caring for yourself also opens you up to being more available for the people you care about. Remember the analogy of the oxygen mask from step 2? The more compassionate you are about your own well-being, the more available you will be to others.

Self-compassion actually enhances relationships, making them stronger and more gratifying. By loving ourselves, we build self-esteem and decrease our tendency to rely on others to meet our emotional needs and validate our worth. In turn, we become less clingy, needy, and dependent, which enriches the quality of relationships all around. When you start by showing love and compassion toward yourself, you simultaneously become more loving toward others.

Here are just a few ways you can show yourself compassion:

- Hug yourself
- Use a sense of humor to laugh at yourself or situations
- Forgive yourself and not be so hard on yourself
- Respond to symptoms of tiredness or stress
- Ask for or schedule a massage
- Get rest when under the weather
- Give yourself a pat on the back
- Acknowledge your own emotions
- Allow yourself to cry
- Tend to your wounds, physical and emotional
- Cut yourself slack
- Give yourself amnesty from past mistakes

Add your own ideas here:

_____

_____

_____

_____

Once you have spent some time brainstorming ways to demonstrate self-compassion, begin putting them into practice. For the next week, make a point every day to practice self-compassion and record one thing that falls into each of the categories in the A Week of Self-Compassion chart on page 194. These things don't need to be grand gestures or major accomplishments; they can be very simple. All that's required is conscious effort and awareness of your intent to act in loving ways that honor who you are and promote an attitude of kindness.

Look Back to Move Forward

In this final step, you've discovered the importance of love directed toward yourself, from yourself. Hopefully, you've begun the challenge of looking in the mirror, into your own eyes, to express the words "I love you," or something like it, every day. Although it may feel ridiculous at first, it does get easier with time. Just like you would want to be silly with a best friend, allow yourself to be silly with yourself as you take small risks to become stronger. Engaging in daily practices of self-love will help rewire your brain as you develop new ways of thinking and behaving. Self-love is about nurturing your spirit, so practice self-loving actions regularly, just like you care for your mind and body.

As you move forward:

Learn to take a compliment. Be cognizant of how you react to compliments, demonstrating self-respect and openness to letting love in by choosing to accept kudos with grace.

Fight off doubt. Continue to replace any self-talk doubting your worthiness of praise with positive messages, and create affirmations that support your willingness to hear and speak loving words.

Keep connections positive. Remember that self-love enhances your relationships with others and allows you to maintain connections that are healthy and fulfilling. Minimize your contact with any abusive people or those who create obstacles to feeling worthy and whole.

Trust in yourself. Use assertiveness to establish and enforce healthy boundaries. Make healthy choices in relationships and interact in ways that support your ability to achieve the best life possible for yourself.

Show compassion. Find ways to express self-compassion and compassion to others through loving actions and willingness to volunteer.

And finally, celebrate your progress as you finish reading this book and contemplate the ways you have grown. Remember that the journey toward loving yourself and improving your self-esteem is an ongoing process that will benefit from continued attention and reflection throughout your entire life.

Write about your biggest takeaways from this chapter and how you can use them to help you build self-esteem:

Think about how it feels to love yourself. Write about your emotions, and reflect on how you can use your feelings to continue moving forward with the healthiest level of self-esteem possible:

A Week of Self-Compassion

	MONDAY	TUESDAY	WEDNESDAY
Something good about today.			
Something I did well today.			
Something I accomplished today.			
Something I'm proud of myself for.			
Something I handled with self-compassion.			
Something I plan to do for myself tomorrow.			

THURSDAY	FRIDAY	SATURDAY	SUNDAY

TAKE ACTION!

1. Say something new, spontaneous, and positive to yourself each day as you look in the mirror.
2. Make a daily intention regarding how you will devote quality time to self-care.
3. Purchase or make a small gift for yourself this week.
4. Determine a boundary you would like to set in a relationship and work toward communicating it with assertiveness skills.
5. Say a simple thank-you in response to any compliments you receive in the next few weeks and write about how doing so made you feel.

Moving Forward

Congratulations! You have made it through the five steps! Hopefully you have developed a greater connection with your own unique identity and have unleashed some of the inner strength that will serve as your most powerful tool moving forward, guiding you as you continue to develop more confidence and greater self-esteem. You have worked hard to tackle some tough issues, achieved a noble goal, and placed yourself well on the path to discovering your true potential.

If you aren't yet feeling complete confidence and solid inner strength, don't let this discourage you. Building self-esteem isn't like flipping on a light switch, and it's not something you do simply by making it to the end of this book; but if you have been diligently completing exercises and practicing the action items from each step, you have likely experienced some shifts in your perspective as your level of self-esteem begins to improve.

Using the same continuum from chapter 1 (page 9), where would you pinpoint your current level of self-esteem today?

SELF-ESTEEM CONTINUUM

Low  High

Has your overall self-esteem improved from where you started out? If so, what rewards are you experiencing as a result? If not, what do you think is impeding your progress? Which suggestions have you tried to incorporate into your life and which of them have been the most helpful? What do you think you can do to help this further along?

_____

_____

_____

_____

_____

_____

Your self-esteem may not yet be quite where you would like it to be, but with an ongoing commitment to using the new tools and skills you've learned, your self-esteem will continue to improve. Even once you reach a solid level of healthy self-esteem consistent across all areas of your life, continue utilizing all of the steps discussed to maintain steady, stable self-esteem.

Remember that life's setbacks can derail your progress, so making a special effort to practice and incorporate each tool into your daily life is vital to ensuring ongoing self-esteem. While our initial work together is nearly done, your journey to sustaining healthy self-esteem will continue on. Remember that maintaining healthy self-esteem requires a lifelong commitment to keeping up with your new ways of relating to, caring for, and appreciating yourself. It will continue to get easier with time and practice as you lock in healthy habits and completely shift your entire way of being to the healthier, happier you we've talked about throughout this book.

This workbook has provided you a space to work through factors that contributed to low self-esteem and process the thoughts and emotions that emerged as you explored new materials. Look back over your responses to the questions and exercises you completed, and consider how things might be different now. In particular, you may find it useful to review the Self-Esteem Checklist in chapter 1 to see whether any of your responses have changed.

What do you notice when you look back and compare where you are now to where you started out?

_____

_____

_____

_____

What areas do you still plan to improve?

_____

_____

_____

_____

As you move on, return to this book as often as you wish. Use it as a reference, and be sure to periodically look back over your work to monitor your growth. Prioritize holding onto your sense of well-being as you navigate your future with a continued effort to fervently practice self-care, self-respect, self-acceptance, and self-love. And please don't be afraid to get help if you ever need it (see Resources, page 201).

Remember to give yourself credit and praise for your progress, including even the smallest of baby steps. You did this! Continue to set goals that are healthy and realistic, and persist in utilizing everything you have learned. Be your own loyal friend. Honor yourself and be ruthless about protecting your self-esteem, like you would that of a good friend. As you have discovered, healthy self-esteem is at the root of all forms of well-being.

Maintaining healthy self-esteem will enable you to value your life and pursue your passions, leading to a happier, more fulfilling existence. It will allow you to feel secure with your identity, no matter what life throws your way. You now have the tools to cultivate your best life and to approach every day with a greater sense of well-being. Your stronger self-esteem will help you to be more resilient than ever. I wish you continued success and peace in your ongoing journey. Remember, you are worth every bit of it!

RESOURCES

FINDING HELP

Search for Therapists & Support Groups

Anxiety and Depression Association of America
ADAA.org

Good Therapy
GoodTherapy.org

Psychology Today
PsychologyToday.com

National Alliance on Mental Illness
NAMI.org

Substance Abuse and Mental Health Services Administration
SAMHSA.gov

Search for Nutritionists & Other Wellness Professionals

Health Professionals Directory
HealthProfs.com

Help Hotlines

Domestic Violence Hotline
800.799.7233

Suicide Prevention Hotline
800.273.8255

Sexual Assault Hotline
800.656.4673

WELLNESS RETREATS

Canyon Ranch
CanyonRanch.com

Kripalu Center for Yoga & Health
Kripalu.org

Miraval
MiravalResorts.com

TREATMENT CENTERS

Brookhaven Retreat
BrookhavenRetreat.com

Lindner Center of HOPE
LindnerCenterOfHope.org

Menninger Clinic
MenningerClinic.com

Orchid Recovery Center
OrchidRecoveryCenter.com

Sierra Tucson
SierraTucson.com

FINDING VOLUNTEER OPPORTUNITIES

America Natural and Cultural Resources Volunteer Portal
Volunteer.gov

Volunteer Match
VolunteerMatch.org

BOOKS & OTHER MEDIA

Assertiveness Training

Alberti, Robert E., and Michael L. Emmons. *Your Perfect Right: Assertiveness and Equality in Your Life and Relationships.* 9th ed. Atascadero, CA: Impact Publishers, 2008.

Bloom, Lynn, and Karen Coburn. *The New Assertive Woman: Be Your Own Person Through Assertive Training.* Rev. ed. Gretna, LA: Selfhelp Success Books, 2003.

Bower, Sharon Anthony, and Gordon H. Bower. *Asserting Yourself: A Practical Guide for Positive Change*. Rev. ed. Cambridge, MA: Da Capo Press, 1991.

Body Image & Eating Issues

Johnston, Anita. *Eating in the Light of the Moon: How Women Can Transform Their Relationships with Food Through Myths, Metaphors, and Storytelling*. Carlsbad, CA: Gürze Books, 2000.

Kilbourne, Jean. *Killing Us Softly 4: Advertising's Image of Women*. [Documentary film]. Northampton, MA: Media Education Foundation, 2010.

Maine, Margo. *Body Wars: Making Peace with Women's Bodies*. Carlsbad, CA: Gürze Books, 2000.

Healthy Relationships & Boundaries

Bloomfield, Harold H. *Making Peace with Your Parents: The Key to Enriching Your Life and All Your Relationships*. Rev. ed. New York: Ballantine Books, 1996.

Engel, Beverly. *Loving Him Without Losing You: How to Stop Disappearing and Start Being Yourself*. New York: John Wiley & Sons, 2000.

Mood Disorders

Bourne, E.J. *The Anxiety & Phobia Workbook*. 4th ed. Oakland, CA: New Harbinger Publications, 2005.

Ilardi, Stephen S. *The Depression Cure: The 6-Step Program to Beat Depression Without Drugs*. Cambridge, MA: Da Capo Press, 2010.

Self-Care & Self-Compassion

Brown, Brené. *Daring Greatly: How the Courage to be Vulnerable Transforms the Way We Live, Love, Parent, and Lead*. New York: Gotham Books, 2013.

Brown, Brené. *The Gifts of Imperfection: Let Go of Who You Think You're Supposed to Be and Embrace Who You Are*. Center City, MN: Hazelden, 2010.

Fontana, David. *Learn to Meditate: A Practical Guide to Self-Discovery and Fulfillment*. San Francisco: Chronicle Books, 1999.

Hay, Louise L. *You Can Heal Your Life*. Carlsbad, CA: Hay House, 1999.

Neff, Kristin. *Self-Compassion: Stop Beating Yourself Up and Leave Insecurity Behind*. New York: Harper Collins, 2011.

Peale, Norman Vincent. *The Power of Positive Thinking*. Rev. ed. New York: Fireside, 2007.

Taylor, Madisyn. *DailyOM: Inspirational Thoughts for a Happy, Healthy, and Fulfilling Day*. Carlsbad, CA: Hay House, 2008.

Science

Arden, John B. *Rewire Your Brain: Think Your Way to a Better Life*. Hoboken, NJ: John Wiley & Sons, 2010.

REFERENCES

Agathangelou, Fay. "How Volunteer Activities Build Self-Esteem." *Healthy Places for Your Mental Health*. Accessed February 5, 2018. www.healthyplace.com /blogs/buildingselfesteem/2015/09/volunteering-to-build-self-esteem/.

Alberti, Robert E., and Michael L. Emmons. *Your Perfect Right: Assertiveness and Equality in your Life and Relationships*. 9th ed. Atascadero, CA: Impact Publishers, 2008.

Arden, John B. *Rewire Your Brain: Think Your Way to a Better Life*. Hoboken, NJ: John Wiley & Sons, 2010.

Beattie, Melody, and Gabrielle De Cuir. *The Language of Letting Go*. Beverly Hills, CA: Phoenix Books, 2009.

Begley, Sharon. "Why Parents May Cause Gender Differences in Kids." *Newsweek*. Accessed January 13, 2017. www.newsweek.com/why-parents-may-cause -gender-differences-kids-79501?rx=us.

Bessenoff, Gayle R. "Can the Media Affect Us? Social Comparison, Self-Discrepancy, and the Thin Ideal." *Psychology of Women Quarterly*, 30, no. 3 (September 2006): 239–51.

Bleidorn, Wiebke, Jaap J. A. Denissen, Jochen E. Gebauer, Ruben C. Arslan, Peter J. Rentfrow, Jeff Potter, and Samuel D. Gosling. "Age and Gender Differences in Self-Esteem—A Cross-Cultural Window." *Journal of Personality and Social Psychology* 111, no. 3 (September 1, 2016): 396-410. doi:10.1037/pspp0000078.

Bloom, Lynn Z. Karen Coburn, and Joan Pearlman. *The New Assertive Woman*. Gretna, LA: Selfhelp Success Books, 2003.

Bourne, Edmund J. *The Anxiety & Phobia Workbook*. 4th ed. Oakland, CA: New Harbinger Publications, 2005.

Bower, Sharon Anthony, and Gordon H. Bower. *Asserting Yourself: A Practical Guide for Positive Change*. Rev. ed. Cambridge, MA: Da Capo Press, 1991.

Branden, Nathaniel. *The Six Pillars of Self-Esteem*. New York: Bantam Books, 1994.

Brown, Brené. Daring Greatly: *How the Courage to Be Vulnerable Transforms The Way We Live, Love, Parent, and Lead*. New York: Gotham Books, 2013.

Brown, Brené. *I Thought It Was Just Me (But It Isn't): Making the Journey from "What Will People Think?" to "I Am Enough."* New York: Avery, 2007.

Brown, Brené. *The Gifts of Imperfection: Let Go of Who You Think You're Supposed to Be and Embrace Who You Are*. Center City, MN: Hazelden, 2010.

Brown, Kevin M., Russell Hoye, and Matthew Nicholson. "Self-Esteem, Self-Efficacy, and Social Connectedness as Mediators of the Relationship Between Volunteering and Well-Being." *Journal of Social Service Research* 38, no. 4 (2012): 468-83. doi:10.1080/01488376.2012.687706.

"Building Self-Esteem: Babies and Children." *Raising Children Network*. Accessed January 10, 2018. raisingchildren.net.au/articles/self-esteem_different _ages.html.

Burns, David D. *Feeling Good: The New Mood Therapy*. New York: Harper, 1980.

Burns, David D. *Ten Days to Self-Esteem*. New York: HarperCollins, 1993.

Burns, David D. *The Feeling Good Handbook*. Rev. ed. New York: Plume, 1999.

Chaves, Robert S., and Todd F. Heatherton. "Multimodal Frontostriatral Connectivity Underlies Individual Differences in Self-Esteem." *Social Cognitive and Affective Neuroscience* 10, no. 3 (March 1, 2015): 364-70. *doi:10.1093/scan /nsu063*.

"Dartmouth Researchers Discover a Source of Self-Esteem in the Brain."
Dartmouth Press Release. June 16, 2014. Accessed January 3, 2018.
www.dartmouth.edu/press-releases/brainselfesteem061614.html.

Dove Campaign for Real Beauty. www.dove.com/us/en/stories/campaigns.html.

Eliot, Lise. *Pink Brain, Blue Brain: How Small Differences Grow into Troublesome
Gaps—And What We Can Do About It.* New York: Mariner Books, 2010.

Engel, Beverly. *Loving Him Without Losing You: How to Stop Disappearing and
Start Being Yourself.* New York: John Wiley & Sons, 2000.

Frankl, Viktor Emil. *Man's Search for Meaning.* Boston: Beacon Press, 2006.

Gallagher, Ann M., and James C. Kaufman. "Gender Differences in Mathematics:
An Integrative Psychological Approach." Accessed January 10, 2018. static1
.squarespace.com/static/550b09eae4b0147d03eda40d/t/5525f80be4b060fb
2f4505b3/1428551691019/math-is-hard.pdf.

"Global Gender Gap Report 2015, The." *World Economic Forum.* Accessed
January 6, 2018. reports.weforum.org/global-gender-gap-report-2015/.

Goldman, Bruce. "Two Minds: The Cognitive Differences Between Men and
Women." *Stanford Medicine.* Accessed January 10, 2018. stanmed.stanford.edu
/2017spring/how-mens-and-womens-brains-are-different.html.

Goswami, Pinky. "Ageing and Its Effect on Body-Self Image, Mood, and Self-
Esteem of Middle Age Women and Older Women." *Journal of Humanities and
Social Sciences* 18, no. 5 (November–December 2018): 63-73. doi:10.9790
/0837-1855373.

Harra, Carmen. "35 Affirmations That Will Change Your Life." *Huffington Post.*
Accessed January 20, 2018. www.huffingtonpost.com/dr-carmen-harra
/affirmations_b_3527028.html.

Hay, Louise L. *You Can Heal Your Life.* Carlsbad, CA: Hay House, 1999.

Heitger-Ewing, Christy. "I took the 21-Day Self-Esteem Challenge and Here's What Happened." *Huffington Post.* Accessed January 10, 2018. www.huffington post.com/christy-heitgerewing/i-took-the-21day-selfeste_b_7617396.html.

Hibbert, Christina. "Hormones and Women's Mental Health." *Healthy Places.* Accessed January 6, 2018. www.healthyplace.com/blogs/yourmentalhealth/2013 /02/hormones-and-womens-mental-health/.

Hurst, Katherine. "Always Over Apologizing for Everything? 5 Ways to Stop Saying Sorry Too Much." *TheLawOfAttraction.com.* Accessed January 20, 2018. www.thelawofattraction.com/stop-saying-sorry/.

Jewell, Louisa. *Wire Your Brain for Confidence: The Science of Conquering Self-Doubt.* Toronto: Famous Warrior Press, 2017.

Johnson, Sharon L. *Therapist's Guide to Clinical Intervention: The 1-2-3's of Treatment Planning.* 2nd ed. San Diego, CA: Academic Press. 2004.

Kilbourne, Jean. *Killing Us Softly 4: Advertising's Image of Women.* [Documentary Film]. Northampton, MA: Media Education Foundation, 2010.

Krantz, Rachel. "The One PMS Symptom Nobody Talks About." *Bustle.* Accessed January 4, 2018. www.bustle.com/articles/134402-the-one-pms-symptom -nobody-talks-about.

Kulkarni, Jayashri. "Chemical Messengers: How Hormones Affect Our Mood." *The Conversation.* Accessed January 6, 2018. theconversation.com/chemical -messengers-how-hormones-affect-our-mood-42422.

Luskin, Fred. *Forgive for Good.* New York: HarperCollins, 2002.

MacCutcheon, Megan. *Building Self-Esteem: A Guide to Achieving Self-Acceptance & a Healthier, Happier Life.* Washington, DC: Balancing Project Press, 2014.

Maine, Margo. *Body Wars: Making Peace with Women's Bodies.* Carlsbad, CA: Gürze Books, 2000.

McLeod, Saul. "Maslow's Hierarchy of Needs." *Simply Psychology*. Accessed January 10, 2016. www.simplypsychology.org/maslow.html.

McQuaid, Michelle. "Wish You Could Banish Self-Doubt?" *Huffington Post*. Accessed January 20, 2018. www.huffingtonpost.com/michelle-mcquaid/wish -you-could-banish-sel_b_7148754.html.

Neff, Kristin. *Self-Compassion: Stop Beating Yourself Up and Leave Insecurity Behind*. New York: HarperCollins, 2011.

Onion, Rebecca. "A New Study Looks at What Becoming a Mother Does to Your Self-Esteem." *Slate.com*. Accessed January 6, 2017. www.slate.com/blogs/xx _factor/2017/07/06/mothers_and_self_esteem.html.

Oprah's Lifeclass. "Oprah and Brené Brown on Vulnerability and Daring Greatly." Season 3, Episode 314. *OWN*. September 22, 2013.

Padilla-Walker, Laura M., Gustavo Carlo, and Madison K. Memmott-Elison. "Longitudinal Change in Adolescents' Prosocial Behavior toward Strangers, Friends, and Family." Journal of Research on Adolescence (November 2017). doi:10.1111/jora.12362.

Peale, Norman Vincent. *The Power of Positive Thinking*. Rev. ed. New York: Fireside, 2007.

Pease, Barbara, and Allan Pease. *Why Men Don't Listen and Women Can't Read Maps*. New York: Broadway Books, 1998.

Pinquart, Martin, and Silvia Sorensen. "Gender Differences in Self-Concept and Psychological Well-Being in Old Age: A Meta-Analysis." *The Journals of Gerontology* 56, no.4 (July 2001): 195–213. doi:10.1093/geronb/56.4.P195.

Roberts, Emily. "How Sleep Impacts Your Self-Esteem." *HealthyPlace.com*. Accessed January 10, 2018. www.healthyplace.com/blogs/buildingselfesteem /2014/04/how-sleep-impacts-your-self-esteem/.

Russello, Salenna. "The Impact of Media Exposure on Self-Esteem and Body Satisfaction in Men and Women." *Journal of Interdisciplinary Undergraduate Research* 1, no. 4 (2009). https://knowledge.e.southern.edu/jiur/vol1/iss1/4.

Schroll, Andrea V. "10 Things You Can Do Today to Overcome Self-Doubt." *Huffington Post*. Accessed January 10. www.huffingtonpost.com/andrea-v-schroll -/10-things-you-can-do-today-to-overcome-self-doubt_b_9777824.html.

Smith, Ann W. *Overcoming Perfectionism: Finding the Key to Balance & Self-Acceptance*. Rev. ed. Deerfield Beach, FL: Health Communications, 2013.

Stern, Denise. "Emotional Symptoms of Low Estrogen." *Livestrong.com*. Accessed January 4, 2018. www.livestrong.com/article/27324-emotional -symptoms-low-estrogen/.

Tousignat, Lauren. "Now There's Proof Thin Models Ruin Your Self-Esteem." *NYPost*. Accessed January 6, 2018. https://nypost.com/2017/08/30/now-theres -proof-thin-models-ruin-your-self-esteem/.

Tugend, Alina. "Praise is Fleeting, but Brickbats We Recall." *The New York Times*. Accessed January 12, 2018. www.nytimes.com/2012/03/24/your-money/why -people-remember-negative-events-more-than-positive-ones.html.

Wall, Cynthia. *The Courage to Trust: A Guide to Building Deep and Lasting Relationships*. Oakland: New Harbinger, 2004.

Warrell, Margie. "Is Self-Doubt Holding Your Back? 5 Ways to Build Confidence and Banish Doubt." *Forbes*. Accessed January 12, 2018. www.forbes.com/sites /margiewarrell/2014/09/18/banish-doubt-build-confidence/.

Werber, Cassie. "*Having Kids Lowers Women's Self-Esteem For at Least Three Years*." *Quartz*, July 2, 2017. https://qz.com/1019876/having-kids-lowers -womens-self-esteem-for-at-least-three-years/.

Whitfield, Charles L. *Boundaries and Relationships: Knowing, Protecting, and Enjoying the Self*. Deerfield Beach, FL: Health Communications, 2010.

Whitley, Bernard E. Jr. "Masculinity, Femininity, and Self-Esteem: A Multitrait-Multimethod Analysis." *Sex Roles: A Journal of Research* 18, no. 78 (April 1988): 419-31. doi:10.1007/BF00288393.

Whitley, Bernard E. Jr. "Sex Role Orientation and Self-Esteem: A Critical Meta-Analytic Review." *Journal of Personality and Social Psychology* 44, no. 4 (April 1983): 765-78. doi:10.1037/0022-3514.44.4.765.

Wilding, Melody. "Three Ways Highly Successful People Handle Self Doubt." *Forbes*. Accessed January 12, 2018. www.forbes.com/sites/melodywilding/2017 /04/05/3-ways-highly-successful-people-handle-self-doubt/#19a802e6789f.

Williams, Joanne M., and Candace Currie. "Self-Esteem and Physical Development in Early Adolescence: Pubertal Timing and Body Image." *The Journal of Early Adolescence* 20, no. 2 (May 1, 2000): 129-49. doi:10.1177 /0272431600020002002.

Zenger, Jack, and Joseph Folkman. "The Ideal Praise-to-Criticism Ratio." *The Harvard Business Review*. Accessed January 12, 2017. https://hbr.org/2013/03 /the-ideal-praise-to-criticism.

INDEX

ACKNOWLEDGMENTS

I would like to thank my family and friends for their love and support, especially my husband for all the proofreading, watching the kids while I focused on writing, and learning to cheer me on with positive affirmations. I'm grateful for the friendships I've made with colleagues and for the invaluable guidance and support I've received from supervisors and mentors. Special thanks to Mary McLaughlin and Amy Weidinger, with whom I share a practice at Vienna Counseling—your collaboration, feedback, and encouragement are always so appreciated. Thank you to Elizabeth Castoria for recruiting me for this project; to Patty Consolazio for her hard work in polishing; and to my editor, Susan Randol, who created the overall vision for these steps, which I hope will help countless women. To all the individuals who have shared their journeys with me, especially those whose stories I shared in this book: Thank you—you have taught me so much and made my work so gratifying.

ABOUT THE AUTHOR

Megan MacCutcheon is a licensed professional counselor with a private practice in Vienna, Virginia. She specializes in working with individuals struggling with issues related to identity, self-esteem, trauma, depression, anxiety, and postpartum mood disorders using cognitive behavioral therapy, EMDR, and mindfulness-based approaches. Megan received her Master of Education in community agency counseling from George Mason University and her Bachelor of Science in communication from Boston University. Megan is a Self-Esteem Topic Expert and regular contributor for the GoodTherapy.org blog.

Find additional resources and learn more about Megan at her website: MeganMacCutcheon.com.

CPSIA information can be obtained
at www.ICGtesting.com
Printed in the USA
BVHW091156191020
591207BV00002B/3